BEING BRIGHT IS NOT ENOUGH

The Unwritten Rules of Doctoral Study

ABOUT THE AUTHOR

Dr. Peggy Hawley holds a Ph.D. from The Claremont Graduate University, Claremont, California, with an emphasis in counseling psychology. She spent twenty years teaching and conducting research at San Diego State University, San Diego, California, and is now Professor Emeritus. As founding director of the Joint Doctoral Program in Education (with The Claremont Graduate University) she served as dissertation chair, committee member, and general academic advisor to many students. In preparing this book she traveled from coast to coast interviewing hundreds of students and dozens of professors whose comments are sprinkled throughout as "real life" examples of major points. Dr. Hawley's background in counseling psychology, her research skills, and her concern for the high dropout rate of Ph.D. students, qualifies her to write this book.

Third Edition

BEING BRIGHT IS NOT ENOUGH

The Unwritten Rules of Doctoral Study

By

PEGGY HAWLEY, Ph.D.

Professor Emeritus, San Diego State University
Formerly, Director of Graduate Programs, College of
Education and Director, Joint Ph.D. Program in
Education with The Claremont Graduate University

CHARLES C THOMAS • PUBLISHER, LTD.
Springfield • Illinois • U.S.A.

Published and Distributed Throughout the World by

CHARLES C THOMAS • PUBLISHER, LTD.
2600 South First Street
Springfield, Illinois 62704

©2010 by CHARLES C THOMAS • PUBLISHER, LTD.

ISBN 978-0-398-07923-9 (hard)
ISBN 978-0-398-07924-6 (paper)

Library of Congress Catalog Card Number: 2009047417

With THOMAS BOOKS *careful attention is given to all details of man-
ufacturing and design. It is the Publisher's desire to present books that are satisfactory as to their physical qualities and artistic possibilities and appropriate for their particular use.* THOMAS BOOKS *will be true to those laws
of quality that assure a good name and good will.*

Printed in the United States of America
CR-R-3

Library of Congress Cataloging-in-Publication Data

Being bright is not enough : the unwritten rules of doctoral
study / Peggy Hawley.
3rd ed.
    p. cm.
  Includes bibliographical references and index.
  ISBN 978-0-398-07923-9 (hard) -- 978-0-398-07924-6 (paper)
  1. Universities and colleges--United States--Graduate work. 2. Doctor
of philosophy degree--United States. I. Title

LB2386.H38 2010
378.1'55--DC22

                                                          2009047417

To Perry

PREFACE

Looking back upon my academic career, one of the memories that brings me the most pleasure are the words students used to pass along to each other, "If you have a problem, go see Peggy Hawley."

My distress at seeing bright students drop out and my interest in social science research combined to provide the impetus for writing this book. On a year-long sabbatical leave I interviewed hundreds of doctoral students and dozens of professors across the nation. Then as professor emeritus, I finally found the time to put my thoughts into words.

Written from a student advocacy perspective, this book is intended to speak to students from a variety of backgrounds. In making the unwritten rules of doctoral study more explicit, I have attempted to be insightful rather than scientific, personal rather than objective, and practical rather than theoretical.

P.H.

ACKNOWLEDGMENTS

The most important facilitator of this book was my husband, Perry, who gave me unwavering support for my efforts, literary and otherwise. My brother, Marvin Martin, who spent his life working in the sciences helped me understand the differences in student experiences compared with those in the social sciences. My friend and colleagues, Larry Feinberg and Emery Cummins, helped me in the areas of empirical research and the protection of human subjects. Patricia and Darwin Slindee gave generously of their time and expertise in data management and everything related to computers. Gooldie Estrella graciously provided computer assistance. Ceci Necoechea, my former assistant and long-time dear friend, contributed to this book in a variety of ways out of her years of experience managing a graduate division. Debi Salmon assisted with reviewing and editing this final edition. Also, kudos to the bright and thoughtful students I have worked with over the years—I received much more than I gave. Thank you to Lauren Clark for the cover design.

CONTENTS

Page

Preface vii

Chapter

1. AN "ABD" (ALL BUT DISSERTATION)
   BEHIND EACH PH.D 3
   The Purpose of This Book 5
   For Whom is This Book Written? 5
   Those Who Drop Out 9
   Those Who Finish 9
   That Entrepreneurial Spirit 17
   Summary 19
   Endnotes 20

2. HOW DOCTORAL STUDY DIFFERS
   FROM PREVIOUS PURSUITS 21
   Differences in Intellectual Demands 21
   Differences in Psychological Demands 24
   From Student to Scholar: A Metamorphosis 29
   Straws in the Wind: A Renewed Interest in Teaching? 31
   Grant-Getting 31
   What Graduates Wished They had Known from the Start 32
   Summary 34
   Endnotes 34

3. CHOOSING A DISSERTATION TOPIC 36
   Dozens of "Right" Topics 37
   The Purpose of a Dissertation 37

When to Look for a Topic 38
Where to Look for a Topic 39
Sources 41
Criteria for Choosing a Topic 46
The Problem Statement 50
Assumptions 51
Summary 52
Endnotes 52

4.   YOUR CHAIR, YOUR COMMITTEE, AND YOU 53
Sequence of Steps 55
Those Rare Individuals, Mentors 55
Desirable Professional Characteristics 58
Desirable Personal Characteristics 60
Effects of "The System" 62
Professors to Avoid 62
"Divorcing" Your Chair 65
Strategies for Finding the Chair You Want 66
Understanding Your Learning Style 68
How to Convince a Professor to Sponsor You 70
Selecting the Rest of the Committee 70
Technical Help 71
Working With Your Chair 74
Summary 78
Endnotes 79

5.   WRITING THE PROPOSAL 80
The Many Functions of a Proposal 80
Dissertation Expectations 83
The Elements of a Proposal 84
Basic Research Concepts 89
Human Subjects 93
Data Gathering 94
Advantages of a Pilot Study 98
Research Ethics and the Protection of Human Subjects 100
Writing Style 102
The Proposal Hearing 103

Summary 106
Endnotes 107

6. THE DISSERTATION 108
   Time, the Irreplaceable Resource 108
   Conducting Your Investigation 112
   Data Management 118
   Common Difficulties and What to do About Them 119
   Dissertations Using Qualitative Methods 123
   Working With Your Committee 126
   Updating the Proposal 126
   Making Sense Out of all Those Data 128
   Writing the Conclusions Section 129
   The Dissertation Abstract 130
   Summary 131
   Endnotes 132

7. DEFENSE OF THE THESIS 134
   Spanish Inquisition or Piece of Cake? 137
   Who Will be There? 139
   Getting Ready 139
   Questions, Questions, and More Questions! 142
   Psychological Preparation 145
   Coming Down the Home Stretch 146
   Summary 147
   Endnotes 148

8. SPOUSES, LOVERS, FAMILIES, AND FRIENDS 149
   Spouses and Lovers 149
   To Wives With Degree-Seeking Husbands 150
   To Husbands With Degree-Seeking Wives 151
   Children with a Degree-Seeking Parent 152
   Family and Friends 152
   Summary 154

Index 157

BEING BRIGHT IS NOT ENOUGH

The Unwritten Rules of Doctoral Study

Chapter 1

AN "ABD" (ALL BUT DISSERTATION) BEHIND EACH Ph.D.

Robed figures stand in line, gowns flapping about their knees and mortarboard tassels fluttering in the spring breeze. At last they hear the long-awaited words from the President of the University. . .

"Upon recommendation of the faculties concerned and by the authority vested in me by the Board of Trustees, I confer upon you the degree of Doctor of Philosophy with all the rights, privileges, and responsibilities appertaining hereunto."

This ancient ceremony is repeated annually in thousands of institutions of higher learning throughout the western world. Heavy with the symbolism of medieval scholarship, the conferral of the degree of Doctor of Philosophy is public acknowledgement that the recipient has successfully pursued and captured academe's highest award, the terminal degree in a particular field of study.

Yet standing behind each smiling graduate is the shadow of another person who also expected to be there on this auspicious occasion, but dropped out somewhere along the way. Are these "shadow people" intellectually inferior to those who stayed the course and received their Ph.D.s? Is the graduation ceremony portrayed here simply an example of Social Darwinism in which only the fittest (brightest) survive?

Some of the Best and the Brightest Drop Out

Most academicians to whom I have put these questions say the answer is "no." One study found little to no academic difference between those who dropped out and those who finished as measured by their Graduate Record Examination scores and undergraduate grades.[1]

Somewhat ruefully, professors acknowledge that many of their best and brightest drop out, not even staying around long enough to take preliminary (qualifying) exams. In fact, the dropout rate is so high (nearly one-half of the students who start doctoral programs) that it has spawned its own acronym, "ABD," or all but dissertation.[1]

This acronym has come to stand for any dropout, regardless of the point at which they leave their studies. Some stop in the middle of course work, some during qualifying examinations, and still others quit just before the dissertation or in the middle of it. No matter where in the process it happens, the loss of such a large proportion of bright scholars-in-the-making is astonishing . . . and also, as this book will show, largely unnecessary.

Consider the case of Michael who talked with me just after returning from a conference of the American Psychological Association where he interviewed for an assistant professorship in counseling psychology at a small college in the northeast.

> My interview went well at first. I had studied under Dr. X who is well-known for his work in social intelligence. That was considered a plus as was my practical experience in the "walk-in" office at the university counseling center. It was when they learned I'd been ABD for four years that everything just fell apart. I tried to explain that there had been some family problems and I fully intended to finish, but I could see they had lost interest.

Mike was living in the "no man's land" inhabited by students who, often for good reason, fail to finish in a timely fashion. Each year of delay increases the danger—the probability that the Ph.D. will remain an unfulfilled dream. In Michael's case, I am happy to report, his wife went to work, he secured a part-time teaching position at a community college and was able to graduate two years later. While he didn't get the position he applied for at the APA conference, he did find one and was happily teaching and working on a research grant, the last I heard.

THE PURPOSE OF THIS BOOK

My purpose in writing this book is to help you earn a Ph.D. instead of having to settle for an "ABD." I write from a student advocacy position, drawing from years of experience in advising doctoral candidates as well as insight gained from interviews conducted with hundreds of students and many professors while preparing material for this book.

Occasionally, I put on my professor's or administrator's hat in an attempt to explain the thinking and aims of academics without abandoning my student advocacy position. I strive to be insightful rather than scientific, personal rather than objective, and practical rather than theoretical. I try to make explicit many of the unvoiced institutional expectations that distinguish doctoral study from other experiences in education, and suggest some coping strategies to reduce the ambiguities that trouble most aspiring Ph.D.s.

FOR WHOM IS THIS BOOK WRITTEN?

This book is written primarily for Ph.D.-seekers in the social and behavioral sciences, the humanities, and such professional fields as education, counseling, and social work. I won't presume to advise those in the sciences, although I suspect there are political and psychological similarities, bureaucracies and humankind being what they are. Some of you may be preparing for careers within academic settings and others in business, industry, foundations, think-tanks or government, any place where the doctorate is an advantage. This book is also intended for professors who want to remember what it felt like to be a student in order to be more sensitive to their own students. In the following pages, I offer many of the suggestions I have made to students in person over a span of 20 years. I draw upon my own experiences as a student, faculty member, dissertation chair, and as a director of doctoral programs.

This Book as a Mentor

My hope is that this book will serve as a kind of mentor to help you meet the challenges ahead with a minimum of stress and even enjoy yourself along the way. It is not unrealistic to promise you moments of joy: a serendipitous research finding that offers new insight into your problem. Usually, a strong sense of kinship develops with fellow students and possibly with some faculty. I think that you find yourself looking at the world differently, all at once realizing you are developing a point of view, a *zeitgeist* that is all your own.

Conditions are improving for non-traditional students, those who have to work and attend school part-time, older people returning to update their skills, minorities and foreign students who have found an academic home in this country. In the past, these groups have tended to be isolated from the communication networks enjoyed by more traditional students. This is a real loss because networks are important socializing agents helping people address the political, social, emotional, and intellectual problems they are likely to encounter on their way to the doctorate. Colleges and universities are gradually becoming aware of the needs of diverse groups and are devising ways to help them. Mentoring programs have been established at some universities providing one-on-one advising at times convenient to the student.

Martha was a newly-appointed assistant professor at a large urban university and we were discussing student-faculty relationships over coffee one morning. Laughing, she confessed her viewpoint had changed since her student days.

> At least now I can talk "from both sides of the desk," as a student and as a prof. A year ago I was a grad student fighting to get a weekly appointment with my chair so I could finish my dissertation before my money ran out. I remember complaining bitterly to my boyfriend that this woman, my advisor, would like the university much better if there were no students here at all.
>
> I swore I'd never forget what it was like being a student and I would always be generous with my time. Well . . . I didn't fully understand how hard an untenured prof has to work to get published and how important publications are to tenure and promotion. The time for research has gotta come from somewhere. So, just like my old advisor; I find myself hurrying through student conferences in order to get back to my writing.

Sparse Rewards for Mentoring

Traditionally, chairing six dissertations has been considered the equivalent of teaching one three-unit class. Professors can then "bank" the units and eventually these can be redeemed for released time from teaching. Most professors would tell you, however, that this is mighty meager compensation for the amount of work involved in supervising dissertations.

A more attractive reward for the faculty is the possibility that a doctoral student will help with the professor's own research by taking over some of the time-consuming work of data gathering, computer entry, statistical analysis, etc. Students can also become more than clerics. As junior partners they can offer fresh insights into the phenomenon being investigated, help write research grants, co-author journal articles, and make presentations at professional conferences. To some extent, a professor is known by the caliber of the students she attracts. Universities could not function without the cadre of bright, energetic doctoral candidates who serve as a back-up for profs who are on the front line of teaching and research. Your potential value to faculty is key to the successful pursuit of your goa. Working with various professors in this way can give you the information you need to decide whom to approach when picking your dissertation committee. Usually the committee is composed with professors with whom you have taken a course and/or with whom you have worked on a research project. The choices are usually obvious. Remember however, that it is possible that one or more of your choices will be too busy to take on another graduate student so it is wise to have alternatives.

Assistantships

The advantages of assistantships are enormous. In addition to the monetary benefits, you have an opportunity to interact with a variety of faculty members and students in a number of fields in addition to your own. Even non-paying assistantships are worth while. They give you entree into the student subculture, a benefit sometimes overlooked. This group can be an emotionally supportive environment. Outsiders, however close to you, cannot fully understand what you are going through. These relationships often last a lifetime. Moreover, the student grapevine is a source of information not to be found in the university catalogue or department brochures. A fellow student's experience with "Dr. Famous," for example, can be invaluable when searching for a dissertation chair. Of course such information must be filtered through your own unique academic and psychological needs and perceptions.

Gradually, as you become established in a department and find a faculty member to chair your dissertation, your sense of security will grow. Even then, however, you cannot afford to trust the management of your academic progress to anyone but yourself. Be assertive without being aggressive and make it your business to keep track of all requirements, procedures, and deadlines. Nothing much will happen unless you make it happen. Above all, don't expect nurturing. In the final analysis, doctoral pursuit is a lonely quest of heart and head.

Doctoral Students' Comments

To augment my own experience, I spent a sabbatical leave interviewing hundreds of students and dozens of professors across the United States. I talked with them in a variety of settings, from large urban universities to small private colleges. Surprised and touched by students' eagerness to share the ups and downs of student life, I was also impressed by their generosity in recounting strategies that had worked for them. In fact, it was they who convinced me that a book written from a student-advocacy viewpoint, going beyond the usual nuts-and-bolts approach, was long overdue.

The words of one student will illustrate a point of view expressed over and over again. Somewhat older than her peers, Claudia lamented the naiveté which characterized earliest stages of her endeavor.

> If only I had been a bit more sophisticated in the beginning, I would have done things quite differently. I'm not saying I would have gone "quick and dirty," as the kids say, but I wouldn't have taken on such a complicated project either. To make matters worse, my advisor took a dim view of older women seeking advanced degrees in sociology, and I realized too late that it was possible to change advisors. Well, I toughed it out and will graduate in June, but I regret not knowing the ropes at the start.

THOSE WHO DROP OUT

Lack of money is not always the reason students leave before acquiring the final prize as illustrated by the fact that students on fellowships do not complete their degrees at a higher-than-average rate (*The Chronicle of Higher Education* 1/16/2004), nor do they drop out because they are incapable academically. Their scores on the Graduate Record Exam and their grades are similar to those who finish. Still, women drop out more often than men, students of color drop out more often than Anglos and Americans drop more often than foreign students.

Often it is simply a matter of fit. The sciences, business and law have lower attrition rates in part because at the very start they link a professor whose research specialties match those of the entering student. They also have shorter, more clearly defined programs. Foreign students have often determined their academic specialty before coming to this country and do very well in the new environment. In contrast, people of color, although academically capable, may come from families who have not attended college and may feel uncomfortable in the strange setting. Those in the humanities and social sciences are given so much latitude that they often feel cast adrift and neglected.

I have focused on the failure of the university system to socialize people properly about the differences between doctoral study and previous experiences in education. As much as I believe this underlies most of the dropout problem, I don't want to oversimplify what I know to be an extremely complex phenomenon.

The doctoral experience is as unique as a fingerprint and failure to do justice to its complexity merely trivializes it. Many reasons for non-completion lie outside the scope of this book: a chair moves to another university; irreplaceable data are lost; an unanticipated child is born; or time and money run out. The decision to quit is not an easy one to make. Whatever the underlying reasons, large numbers of students simply lose forward momentum and drift away, avoiding the painful *conscious* decision to quit. In fact, an astonishing number comtinue to pay tuition semester after semester rather than face the hard reality that they are not going to acquire the degree they so enthusiastically set out to earn.

The problem is rarely lack of commitment. Most enter Ph.D. programs with strong feelings of dedication and great eagerness to realize a cherished dream. Promising scholars at the start, they become discouraged before acquiring the sophistication to cope with their new environment.

The Doctorate is a Terminal Degree

Unfortunately, the Ph.D. is a terminal degree in more than one sense. It is almost a given that those who do not complete it within the allotted time never make another attempt. Few other serious undertakings in life offer only a single shot at success. Marital failure does not preclude other matrimonial adventures, nor does bankruptcy foreclose future business options. Yet, it is rather for anyone who has failed in their first attempt for a doctorate to try again. For one thing, institutions do not encourage one to try again, and, for another, people are usually so disheartened that they cannot bear to start the process all over again.

As rare as successful second attempts are, I want to emphasize that success the second time around is not impossible. I have known students who changed committees, stayed at the same university, and earned their degrees. I have also known students who changed universities and were successful in a new setting. Needless to say, it saves time, money, and psychic investment to capture the prize the first time around. This book is dedicated to helping you do just that.

The Magnitude of the Problem

Concerned over the loss of doctoral students in the humanities and social sciences, two large urban universities investigated this phenomenon in 1989. They discovered that slightly over half of their doctoral students stayed on to earn the Ph.D. and concluded that lack of proper mentoring was a major factor in the students' decisions to abandon their studies.[2]

Two years later, the Mellon Foundation undertook a massive national study of 35,000 students from ten leading universities. They looked at an enormous number of issues influencing the student attrition rate and time taken to complete the degree.[3]

All of these investigations came to similar conclusions, that about half of the doctoral students in the humanities and social sciences drop out and that the nurturing of students by faculty mentors is extremely important. Mentoring was cited as a major factor in the varying rates of attrition and length of time-to-degree.

The fact that ABDs are a substantial minority in American society doesn't appear to have troubled anybody very much, least of all the academy. I infer this lack of concern from the relative lack of information gathered on dropouts at the doctoral level. Today, an awakening interest can be seen.

THOSE WHO FINISH

In 2008 the Ph.D. Completion Project was established to address issues surrounding Ph.D. completion and attrition. This seven-year project was funded by Pfizer Inc. and the Ford Foundation. Participants included 29 major universities in the U.S. and Canada.

The Project demonstrated that under favorable conditions all entering students have the academic ability to complete the doctorate. Still, no more than three-fourths of the students stay on long enough to complete their degrees.

Statistics from the 1991 National Research Council (Summary Report Doctorate Recipients from United States Universities)[4] show large differences among fields in the time it took students to finish. Engineers finished most quickly with an average of 6 years in "registered time," which is the period in which they were continuously enrolled. Humanities students took the longest, 8.3 years in registered time. When the time-to-degree included periods when students were not formally registered, it was the physical sciences students who completed their studies most quickly, averaging 7.6 total years, and the education students who took the longest, averaging almost 18 years. Obviously, having a master's degree cut an average of two years off completion time in all fields.

As the survey points out, these differences are partly a reflection of the financial support available in the sciences and engineering, and the lack of it in humanities and education. Graduating engineers reported the lowest percentage of debt and social science graduates reported the highest. Time-to-degree differences may also reflect differences in support at the department level where social science and humanities students are less likely to have mentors and must search for ways to compensate for this deficiency.

Key factors affecting the likelihood of finishing are in order of importance:

1. Selection (fit between student and area of study)
2. Mentoring (access to faculty)
3. Financial Support
4. Program Environment (comfort level)
5. Research Mode of the field. (research skills)
6. Processes and Procedures. (access to information)

Work Settings

What kinds of work settings will graduates enter and what skills will they need to succeed? The Ph.D. is an entrée into many different environments, anywhere people with skill and intellect are needed. We can agree that successful people will need to be intelligent, but what exactly does that mean? Let us examine what we mean by *intelligence.*

Robert Steinberg has done extensive work on intelligence and its implications for success. His early work focused on the differences between "test smarts" and "street smarts" and the term *street smarts* have become part of the common lexicon. He noticed that there were many occasions when those with higher IQs failed at an important task while those with lower IQs succeeded. Intrigued by these findings, he began to search for new ways to describe intelligence. The time-honored definition of intelligence as (1) a single entity measured by a test in the classroom or laboratory, (2) restricted to right and wrong, and (3) divided into linguistic and math areas is out of date. These definitions are inadequate to explain why one succeeds or fails in the university or in daily life. Released from antiquated ways of thinking, he and other researchers began to expand the construct into different kinds of intelligences. Howard Gardner is another researcher who has investigated intelligence. A professor at Harvard, he specializes in social relationships. He found seven different modes or ways of interacting intelligently with the environment: linguistic, logical/mathematical, musical, bodily/kinesthetic, spatial, interpersonal and intrapersonal (Frames of Mind, 1983).

Management Styles

Just as the notion of intelligence has been expanded there has been growing recognition that successful managers follow a different model than those in the past (*Time*, The Future of Work, May 25, 2009). They employ what is called a *transformational* leadership style. Instead of being confrontational they are conciliatory, instead of being competitive they are consensus builders. They focus on the long-term and the good of the organization. Self-awareness and knowledgeable about their own emotions, they have strong personalities and are less vulnerable to manipulation by others.

Jess Hardin appeared to be one of the most promising employees Klondike Computer Systems had ever hired. The reasons for his leaving his previous employer were unclear, but management was so impressed by his confident presentation and straight A grades that they hired him for a supervisory position on the spot.

A few months into the job he was showing a new employee around the plant. Their last stop was at the bookkeeper's office. Looking over her shoulder he noticed that she was sending out a duplicate bill. He pointed this out and she apologized and promised that it would never happen again.

Hardin snapped, "Well see that it doesn't young lady."

Hardin's lack of social skills is painfully obvious. He could have pointed out her mistake less harshly or, better yet, waited until they were alone. He should have called her by name instead of the patronizing "young lady." His remarks were both sexist and ageist. The larger problem was that his manner affected more than just the two of them. Word of the incident spread throughout the organization and had a bad affect on morale.

The Gender Gap

Nationally, women earn 45 percent of the doctorates but are still underrepresented in engineering and the sciences in spite of showing gains in biology. There, the percentage of women graduate students grew from 39 percent in 1986 to 45 percent in 1995 (The New Majority: CGS/GRE Survey Results Trace Growth of Women in Graduate Education). Across all disciplines women are continuing to rise. This trend is most pronounced among Hispanics, African Americans and those from low income families. While this gain is substantial, it must be remembered that a higher percentage of women are engaged in part-time study, 55 percent versus 46 percent for men. This is not an isolated phenomenon. It has been observed across all disciplines and degree programs. Some universities are recognizing the fact that many women are raising families and going to school at the same time. Princeton, for example, has established day care centers in an attempt to help women balance both work and family (*Washington Week*, 2006).

The number of international students receiving Ph.D.s has increased. They now receive 41 percent of the of science and engineering doctorates given by U.S. universities. Males dominate in engineering, math, science and computer science (*Washington Week*, 2006).

Still, stereotypes continue to hinder the entrance of women into traditionally male fields of study. Young women especially shy away from fields such as science, engineering, and information technology, the very fields where the opportunities are greatest for qualified women.

One high school student summed it up for me. "I would like to study computer science but I don't want to be seen as a 'computer geek'."

Increase of Formerly Underrepresented Groups

The efforts of colleges and universities in the United States to attract non-traditional students seems to be paying off. Underrepresented groups are actually growing faster than any other group, especially Asian and Hispanic/Latino women (Council of Graduate Schools, 1997).

African American women form the largest minority group in graduate education today. They account for 46 percent of minority women in graduate programs and 26 percent of the total minority enrollment. Hispanic women comprise the next largest group, followed by Asian American men.

Business schools are especially successful in attracting and retaining students who have not been well-represented in the past. They also make an effort to hire minority professors, aware that their mere presence has an encouraging effect on students. One project conducts a nationwide marketing campaign to identify minorities willing to leave their jobs to return to academe in pursuit of a Ph.D. Equally impressive, they have a remarkably low drop-out rate, 25 percent compared to 50 percent in most fields (*The Network Journal*, April 2001).

Older Students

There is evidence that the average age of doctoral students is increasing ("Pursuit of the Ph.D.," *Educational Policy Analysis Archives*, Volume 3 Number 16, 1995). In 1993, the median age of all doctoral recipients was 34.1 years compared with 33.6 in 1987. The field with the highest median age was Education, at 43.0 years, while Chemistry students were the youngest with a median of 29.7 years.

Students beyond the age of 25, are among those categorized as "non-traditional" along with minorities, those born in foreign countries and students who are the first in their families to seek a college education. Their numbers have been increasing in recent years. Non-traditionals average 42.5 years of age as compared with 35.5 years for "traditionals." Those who are first in their families to attend college may have come from families where higher education was considered unimportant or beyond their financial means. There are also subtle cultural pressures operating. Even if unspoken, the notion that *girls don't need to go on to college* remains a powerful influence. Lack of mentors and role models are also inhibiting factors (What Professors They Wish They'd Had. *The Network Journal: Black Professionals and Small Business Magazine*, April 2001).

Often the desire for a college degree comes after several years of experience in the world of work. There's nothing like time in a dead-end, tedious job to make one look for new opportunities. Often change is difficult. Older students are more apt to have to combine school and work and this involves sacrifice for all concerned. Although this is changing, non-traditional students and women are still less likely to receive assistantships and fellowships than their traditional doctoral colleagues (Education Policy Analysis Archives, 1995).

The gender gap between African American males and females is striking. Black women have made far greater educational and career advances than have their male counterparts. Of the individuals reaching the professional management category today, 24 percent are women and only 17 percent are men. While black women don't yet out-earn black men, the educational-achievement gap is evident and still growing (The Black Gender Gap, *Newsweek*. March 3, 2003). Twenty-five percent of young black males go on to college, compared with 35 percent of the women. In high school males are encouraged to be athletes, not scholars, yet rarely make it to the big time sports. Some African women claim that females tend to go higher because they can't depend upon anyone else to support them. They go out into the world with a sense of purpose and often have a strong mother figure to set an example.

The gender gap makes black women ask, "Where are all the good black men? Must I resign myself to remaining childless and unfulfilled, or should I marry someone who is several steps below me on the career ladder? Can I thrive if my brother does not?" There is evidence of serious trouble with marriages when the wife was the dominant wage earner (The Black Gender Gap, *Newsweek*, March 3, 2003). The most encouraging prediction is that black women are weathering a period of transition and will find a way to balance marriage, family and career successfully.

Talented Hispanic women need to be encouraged to prepare for professional fields by attending college. A recent study by The American Association of University Women found that Hispanic women have a higher high school dropout rate than any other group of women, hence are least likely to go on to school. Hispanic women from the ages of 16 to 24 have a 30 percent dropout rate compared to 12.9 percent of black women, and 8.2 percent of white women (The American Association of University Women. *Hispanic Women in Education*, EURWEB, Feb. 5, 2001).

The researchers who conducted this study suggest that Latinas face obstacles not usually encountered by other groups. Cultural pressures from family, boyfriends and fiancées who don't want girlfriends and wives to be *too educated* are a negative influence. If Hispanic women are to succeed, educators and educational administrators need to pay closer attention to bright women and encourage those who would benefit by continuing their education.

BEING BRIGHT IS NOT ENOUGH

I began this chapter with the assertion that successful pursuit of the doctorate requires more than the kind of brains which have served you so well up to now. As this chapter draws to a close, let me describe in greater detail the kind of "smarts" I think you will need to capture the final prize.

As mentioned before, researchers have noticed that people with modest IQs often succeed when those with higher IQs fail in the same or similar situations. Now we know that intelligence is multifaceted and not always captured by standardized tests, i.e., "book learning." Daniel Goleman (Bantam Books, 1995) drawing on brain and behavioral research also asks us to consider different ways of being smart. Emotional intelligence is probably most important when interacting with other people. It includes "self-awareness, impulse control, persistence, zeal, self motivation, empathy and social deftness."

Shipman and Kay (Womanomics, June, 2009, The Future of Work, *Time*, May 25, 2009) suggest that one reason women are finding employment more readily than men is that modern society demands a different behavioral style. Instead of the model that worked previously: the masculine hard-driving, risk-taking style, there is evidence to suggest that successful people now need a more "feminine" approach. This style tends to be less competitive, more consensus-building and conciliatory. I called it a more *feminine* approach as a kind of shorthand. Certainly it has been more typical of women in the past, but the past is past. Men need not avoid this way of relating to people out of fear of being emasculated. This style is simply better related to the modern scene. Moreover, it takes a man sure of his masculinity to change his behavior to a style previously employed by women.

Successful people of both genders in all walks of life seem to have a characteristic that can be labeled "savvy" or "street smarts." They are not only intelligent, they are *shrewd, canny, sharp, cunning,* and *perceptive.* They have learned to read the environment and to manipulate it in order to achieve their legitimate academic ends. They use facts but are not constrained by them and they refuse to view factual data as immutable, tending instead to challenge existing dogma. As thinkers, they recognize the cadence of their own "drummer" when they hear it but are realistic enough to know there are times when it isn't expedient to march to its beat. Finally, street smart people have the self-knowledge to capitalize on their strengths and compensate for their weaknesses and seem to have a knack for finding the right people to help them along their way.

Describing someone as "bright" or "intelligent" is somewhat misleading because it seems to imply a dichotomy, some of us have it and some of us don't. This notion is further reinforced by the concept of intelligence as an indwelling *entity* instead of a *behavior*, something people *have* instead of something people *do.* Having long recognized that individuals differ in their abilities (some excel in math, others in painting, cooking, or mechanics), we still tend to oversimplify this mysterious and important human characteristic.

Robert Sternberg, quoted earlier, approaches the study of intelligence with a common-sense practicality that is as compelling as it is refreshing. He talks about three aspects of intelligence: test smarts, creativity, and street smarts. Test smarts gets you high scores on the GRE and into grad school. This shows you excel at contrived tasks that require speed, good recall, and a high degree of accuracy, *but it doesn't tap your divergent thinking skills or ability to create new ideas.*[5]

Test smarts become *less and less predictive* of success in graduate school as the need for creativity increases. Sooner or later you will have to create something on your own rather than simply follow or imitate the work of others. Finally, in order to advance your ideas and carve out your own professional niche, you must be sophisticated enough to "play the game" according to the rules of the particular setting in which you find yourself. In other words you will need *street smarts.* In this respect, doctoral study shares many of the characteristics of the "real" world outside of academia where problems do not come artificially in orderly progression, each building logically upon the one before. *Instead, problems come helter skelter, often before you as a problem-solver are fully equipped to deal with them.*

THAT ENTREPRENEURIAL SPIRIT

At the risk of offending the purists among you who might resent the analogy, I use the term *entrepreneur* because it illustrates the point I have been making in various contexts throughout this book.

Webster defines an entrepreneur as a person who "organizes, manages, and assumes the risks of a business." What better definition could we find to describe a Ph.D. student? Both the risks and the rewards of the venture are yours and nearly everything you do affects the bottom line. Manage people? Of course you manage people. Not in the sense that you dictate to your fellow students, your chair, or committee members, but in the sense that your attitudes and behaviors directly affect these relationships, and with them, your academic future. Your doctoral committee, these 3 to 5 people, have the power to grant or refuse to grant your doctorate. There are few conditions in life when your future depends on so few. However, today's classmates and faculty advisors can become powerful allies tomorrow, part of a working network that can enhance or inhibit your career.

Self-Management

Self-management is more important now than it has ever been before in your academic life. As the old saying goes, "I have met the enemy, and he is me!" What this aphorism lacks in grammar it makes up for in common sense. The one person in the best position to help or hinder your forward motion is you. Without pushing this analogy any farther, let me note that the high mortality rate in small businesses in America is roughly equivalent to the high dropout rate among doctoral students . . . and for many of the same reasons.

Strive to strike a balance between a cavalier attitude, which underestimates the magnitude of the task ahead, and an unrealistically perfectionist view; they both stifle progress. Without grasping the full range, size and significance of the quest for a Ph.D., you are inclined to put forth too little effort. This is an inhospitable environment for procrastination, careless execution, hasty and unwarranted conclusions. Such behaviors will earn you a reputation for incompetence that, once acquired, is difficult to live down.

Tom was a student I knew well. More articulate than most of his peers, he had sailed through a master's degree without any trouble at all. As good at writing as he was at talking and brimming with ideas, he had gotten in the habit of meeting deadlines by the skin of his teeth. By chance, I met him in the hall just after his dissertation proposal had been turned down by the committee. His first comments showed more than a little youthful arrogance.

> Maybe I didn't act scared enough. I know profs don't like it when you are too sure of your\self. They want you to realize how important the doctorate is and how wise and scholarly they are.
>
> I must admit, my proposal did have some last minute changes that didn't quite fit with the rest of it, although the new ideas were nothing short of brilliant (nervous laughter)! To make a long story short, they want me to rewrite my proposal and go through another hearing after the Christmas break.

Although Tom may have a point about appearing too self-confident (cocky?), it doesn't pay to be a cavalier about the importance of the dissertation. On the other hand, it is a mistake to expect your dissertation to change western civilization as we know it. Saving the environment or discrediting the theory of evolution is beyond the scope of a doctoral investigation. Tackle a feasible project which will make a modest contribution to your field of study and get on with it. The explosion of knowledge in the last century has meant that the Renaissance Man has given way to the Specialist Person who can be comfortable within relatively narrowly defined boundaries of inquiry.

You are about to embark upon a great adventure. In your successful quest for the Doctor of Philosophy Degree in your chosen field, you will be joining a community of scholars who share an ancient and honorable tradition. At least in an *ideal* sense, scholars all over the western world are committed to a number of basic values, the most fundamental of which is the pursuit of truth (to the extent that truth can be known) even when it is inconvenient, politically unpopular, and flies in the face of established dogma.

SUMMARY

This book is intended to help students earn a Ph.D. instead of an ABD. Half of doctoral students drop out, not because they aren't bright enough, but because they aren't sophisticated in the ways of academe. I am sorry to admit that the academy does little to ameliorate this view. What I say here is drawn from 25 years in graduate education–as a student, professor, dissertation supervisor, and Director of Graduate Programs. It is also enlivened by hundreds of interviews with doctoral students across the United States.

I have concluded that successful students must have more than "book smarts," they must also have *street smarts*. This means they must be tough (intellectually and emotionally), politically savvy, disciplined, and able to accurately read the environment in which they have to function.

NOTES

1. Sternberg's estimate of a 50 percent dropout rate was later confirmed by studies designed to capture this statistic. He attributes much failure to lack of support at the doctoral level-support which is available to students at lower levels of education. See Sternberg, David: *How to Complete and Survive a Doctoral Dissertation*. New York, St. Martin's Press, 1992.
2. One of the few studies conducted by a university administrative body on Ph.D. dropouts was done by Narad & Cerny of the Graduate Division of the University of California at Berkeley. Comparing their completion rates with the University of Michigan at Ann Arbor, they found them similar. Both at Berkeley and at Michigan slightly more than half of all doctoral students (UCB 52%, UM 54%) completed their degrees. Narad, M.and J. Cerny, *From Facts to Actions: Expanding the Educational Role of the Graduate Division*. Fourteenth Annual Meeting of the Association for the Study of Higher Education, Atlanta, Georgia, November 2–5, 1989.
3. The Mellon Foundation sought answers to a number of major questions from a comparison of completion rates among fields of study to the state of the job market. The last part of the book contains recommendations for policy changes, especially in the social sciences and humanities. Bowen W.G. and N.I. Rudenstine: *In Pursuit of the Ph.D.* Princeton, New Jersey: Princeton University Press, 1992.
4. These statistics came from the National Science Foundation and National Research Council Summary Reports of U.S. Universities for the years 1989, 1990, and 1991. See *Summary Report: Doctorate Recipients from United States Universities*. Washington, D.C. The National Research Council's Office of Scientific and Engineering Personnel, National Academy Press.
5. This article was intended for general audiences interested in Robert J. Sternberg's ideas on intellectual functioning. Entitled, "Three Heads are Better Than One," it was written by R. J. Trotter and published in *Psychology Today*, August, 1986. Also see Sternberg, R. J.: *Beyond IQ A Triarchic Theory of Human Intelligence*, New York: Cambridge University Press, 1985.

Chapter 2

HOW DOCTORAL STUDY DIFFERS FROM PREVIOUS PURSUITS

A doctoral degree is not simply a bigger and better master's degree but an undertaking of an entirely different order. For the sake of discussion, I have separated differences between doctoral study and previous educational experiences into two categories: *intellectual and psychological.* The distinction is somewhat arbitrary because thinking and feeling are likely to be experienced simultaneously in daily life. Thoughtful people invest emotionally in ideas that are important to them and when they do, feelings become the driving force behind rational thinking. Still, discussing them separately will help explain the demands of doctoral study that set it apart from other academic endeavors.

DIFFERENCES IN INTELLECTUAL DEMANDS

In most disciplines, the Ph.D. is considered a research degree and this means that its primary purpose is not to prepare practitioners, clinicians, or teachers, but to produce scholars. If you want to be considered a scholar you must do research. This calls for a major transition in how you think and what you do. As a colleague of mine says, "it requires you to change from being merely a *consumer* of research to becoming a *producer* of research as well." Heretofore, you were expected to inculcate what others had discovered; now, you will be expected to generate knowledge on your own. At times you will be building upon a data base constructed by previous investigations, and at other times you may be challenging the very foundation of current doctrine by starting off in a completely new direction. The heady thought of "seeking the truth wherever it may lead" will necessarily be tempered by the knowledge that there is no escape from evaluation and accountability.

Clearly, your research findings are of little value until they are disseminated to appropriate audiences. Only when your work is published in a "refereed" or "juried" journal will it contribute to your standing as a scholar. As you probably know, these are journals in which manuscripts have been evaluated by an editorial board and have survived fierce competition with other submitted articles. Interestingly, professional journals in social science fields usually don't pay authors for their manuscripts. Publishers assume that adding another article to the writer's curriculum vita is payment enough, and apparently, they are right. This one-sided arrangement is hard for my writer friends outside the university to understand, yet the practice is quite acceptable in the academic world where competition to get published is so keen that some journals accept less than 25 percent of the manuscripts they receive.

The dissertation is not only a rite of passage into this world of scholarship, it can be mined for years to come as a source of ideas for grant applications, journal articles, conference presentations, and topics for classes and seminars. Some students decide to try to capitalize on the enormous effort that went into writing the dissertation by turning it into a book. Occasionally, a dissertation-cum-book gets published, yet it is only fair to warn you that dissertations are not easily converted into book form. Editors complain that most have narrow appeal because the only audience they are directed toward is the student's dissertation committee. This means the typical dissertation is "over-documented, ponderous, and written in 'dissertationese' instead of 'humanese'."[1] In most cases it must be completely rewritten in order to have any chance of publication. If you are determined to convert your dissertation into a book, I suggest that you write a rough book draft at the same time you are writing the dissertation, if you can afford to spend the extra time.

Indifferent Faculty

Early in my data-gathering tour of the United States, a faculty member of an elite northeastern university arranged for me to meet with a group of doctoral candidates. Introducing me as someone interested in "The Lives and Times of Ph.D. Candidates," he left the room. There I was, faced with a somewhat cynical, but curious, roomful of students. Briefly, I explained my purpose and assured complete anonymity for those willing to share their experiences. It took several minutes of discussion for the skepticism to dissipate but the need to air frustrations finally overcame students' reticence and they warmed to the topic. One man, who had just had his proposal rejected, lamented:

> My basic complaint is that nobody around here seems to give a damn. I'm a good student and I know something about research, yet right now I am floundering. I did an empirical investigation for my master's, yet it was nothing like this. Then I had several topics to choose from, a rough outline to follow, and someone to help me with the stats.
>
> In this program I really feel abandoned by the faculty. I submitted my proposal to the prof who was most knowledgeable about my area, only to be told that it wasn't focused enough, whatever that means. Now it looks like she isn't interested. Sure, I'll revise it and try again but I'm really discouraged. To be honest, I thought it *was* focused.

Laissez Faire Versus the Apprenticeship Model

No wonder students feel abandoned. In the social sciences and humanities, true to our democratic principles, we academics follow a laissez faire model of student oversight (no pun intended). Our practice is to allow great latitude in the choice of a topic but to provide very little guidance in determining its feasibility. We expect inexperienced researchers to select a topic from among a bewildering array of possibilities, convince a faculty member of its merit, and then to write an original treatise with an encyclopedic review of prior studies in the field.

This is changing to some extent; the recent trend is toward shorter, "meatier" dissertations with even shorter very pertinent literature reviews. Advisors are telling students to aim at a more realistic goal which challenges them to add a *modest* amount to the body of knowledge in their field of study and demonstrate their ability to conduct independent research, albeit with faculty help when appropriate.

Research in the humanities and social sciences isn't easy. It usually takes place in natural settings (in contrast to laboratories) where extraneous influences present numerous threats to reliability and validity. Research designs must be well-conceived and hypotheses often require sophisticated statistical techniques to shed light on the problem. Many students have not had the courses or the experience to prepare them for this task.

In contrast, doctoral programs in the sciences typically follow an apprenticeship model where students work under close faculty supervision on a project supported by a foundation grant. Each student is assigned a relatively narrow and well-defined piece of the investigation and becomes a member of a team working elbow-to-elbow. Under these conditions, errors of procedure, judgment, and omission are caught before large amounts of time and effort are wasted.

This is not to say that the apprenticeship model is without flaws. Students are denied the thrill of following their own interests and hunches and the close supervision may stifle creativity. A number of students I interviewed said they felt exploited by having to follow the department's research agenda instead of their own. They readily acknowledged, however, that their paths were well-marked and relatively free from ambiguity. Both models have their advantages and there are departments that manage to combine the best features of each.

DIFFERENCES IN PSYCHOLOGICAL DEMANDS

Another important difference between doctoral study and experiences at lower levels of education is in the nature and intensity of psychological demands. It is understandable that academics view the cognitive realm as their primary domain and intellectual accomplishment as their primary mission. Few would argue with this focus.

Nevertheless, there are vast differences among faculty in the degree to which they recognize the psychological components implicit in an undertaking of this kind. It is the *subjectively painful* experiences that underlie most students' decision to quit, yet many doctoral faculties refuse to concern themselves with what they see as non-cognitive matters. Curiously, the higher they rise in their professions, the more cerebral some become and the more disparaging of the emotional components of learning.

A colleague, upon hearing about the book I was writing, remarked with some heat, "Students' emotional states are their own business, not mine. Let grammar school teachers worry about self-concept and such nonsense. Feelings are extraneous to the real business of earning a Ph.D. because a doctorate is granted on the basis of what people know, not how they feel."

While completely missing the point, this comment demonstrates a prevailing attitude, that emotions are "soft" and cognition is "hard" and being hard is better than being soft! When students' emotional states are considered at all, it is assumed that emotional suffering is not only inevitable, it is actually good for them. I don't know whether this is some form of latent Puritanism (if it hurts, it must be good for you) or an indirect way of getting even for one's own travails as a student. I do know adherents of this philosophy seem to equate caring with coddling. One well-published, dignified old-timer declared that he had gone through bloody hell writing his dissertation and wasn't about to hold any student's hand. "Besides," he added, "a little suffering is good for 'em."

Drawing a parallel between caring and coddling, although pervasive, is naive. The truth is that professors don't coddle their most talented students, those in whose work they have the heaviest professional and personal investment. On the contrary, the best students are urged, pushed, prodded, and held to far more exacting standards than their less competent counterparts. Yet the myth prevails and many profs take fierce pride in their reputations for being "hard-nosed" with students.

Not all Faculty are Indifferent

Softening the effect of those with a single-minded focus on things cerebral, are profs who realize that people learn best when they are engaged both emotionally and intellectually. They actually enjoy helping fledgling scholars try their wings. If you can find such a person to sponsor you, your path will be smoothed considerably.

Ann, a candidate for a Ph.D. in education administration, was one of the fortunate ones who found a mentor, although she confessed that the relationship didn't always match the ideal she had in mind.

There are still times when I hate Carol, especially when she tears apart a chapter that I am particularly proud of. Sure, I know she is not attacking me personally. At least I understand it in my head, if not always in my gut.

I have to admit that her toughness really paid off last week when I had my mid-point review. This is the halfway mark when we have to defend our research design with evidence and logic. If you are one of hers, she puts you through a very intense dress rehearsal-she tries to break down everything you say. It takes a lot of her time but after that, the real thing is a breeze. Unless you're one of hers, you don't get the benefit of this coaching.

The point of this discussion is to emphasize that the journey you are beginning is more than an intellectual one, it is an intensely emotional, ego-threatening venture within a highly charged political environment. The sad truth is that the ranks of ABDs are filled with intelligent, but politically naive, people who failed to learn how to negotiate their way past their dissertation committees.

Coping With Double Messages

A major problem with the doctoral environment is that it is fraught with double messages. One day you are treated as a colleague and the next day as a "go-fer," sometimes by the very same person! You follow a promising hunch and are praised by a committee member only to be chastised by your chair for venturing too far out on your own. Having lost the support you enjoyed as an undergrad and not yet achieved the independence you expected as a doctoral candidate, you need great tolerance for ambiguity to cope with the situation. This requires a tough and resilient ego that is not easily bruised and can bounce back quickly after setbacks.

Some cope by saying to themselves, "If I can learn to play the game, I'll get through this." While it may sound cynical, I must admit there are game-playing aspects to earning a Ph.D. The first rule is that you accept the role of a neophyte . . . a talented, creative, and motivated neophyte, but a neophyte nevertheless. Such a role is probably most distasteful to the person who has held a position of authority in the outside world and must quickly adjust to the relatively powerless status of a student.

A Ph.D.-seeking high school principal, on leave from her position, describes her sense of vulnerability and resentment:

> I experienced culture shock when I stepped on this campus. In my job I feel confident and in control . . . sure that I am good at what I do. Now I go through times when I am inarticulate, unsure of my ideas, and even unable to spell correctly. This place turns an adult into a child. It punishes the brash ones who are capable of striking out in fresh directions. I have finally learned, at great psychic cost, to sit at the feet of my "master" and just bide my time until I can be myself again.

At this point you might object, aren't tough-mindedness and independent thinking the marks of a superior intellect and isn't the university exactly the place to exercise these qualities? The answer to this question is a qualified yes. Most profs value precocious, assertive students who exercise reasonable judgment, who know when to stand their ground and when to beat a hasty, but dignified retreat.

Of course, no set of rules can substitute for personal judgment, for each situation is unique and the chemistry between people is essentially unpredictable. In doctoral pursuit, as in most other endeavors, successful people are sensitive to the interpersonal "vibes" which they use to guide them through close encounters with important others. If you find yourself in the hands of an unusually authoritarian chair or committee, you can be comforted by the knowledge that once you are a professor in your own right, you will be relatively free to profess anything you wish. Until then, like the principal, you may just have to bide your time.

Dangers of Timidity and Passivity

On the other hand, excessive timidity and passivity are even more common and considerably more counter-productive than being too aggressive. I have known students who, fearing to bother their sponsors, let months go by, struggling alone with a problem that could have been solved in a 15-minute face-to-face discussion. It is a mistake to appear too tentative in presenting a point of view, and equally unwise to be defeated by an advisor's disapproval when a little assertiveness could make your case. *Intellectual combat is a way of life in universities.* As a doctoral student you need to unlearn the passive conditioning acquired in previous years of schooling and adjust to the challenge-and-defend atmosphere of higher education.

In short, doctoral study is not for the faint-hearted. You have a right and an obligation to present your point of view without apology, even when it is a dissenting one. The trick is, of course, to get the timing right and to distinguish really important issues from relatively unimportant ones.

Jerry, whom I interviewed in a small liberal arts college, told me how he decided to take the bull by the horns after suffering weeks of indecision.

> My chair kept changing his mind and it was driving me crazy. Each time he read a new draft of my proposal, he suggested changes. I finally started taking notes at our meetings so I would be certain of what was said, especially when we talked about research design.
>
> Then yesterday, he told me to go back to the very same statistical procedures I'd put in the original proposal. This time I'd had it! I pulled out my notes and showed him where he had OK'd the procedure he now wanted to change. I thought he'd be mad, since he was a new faculty and all. To my surprise, he just laughed and suggested that we call in the department statistician for advice. Things have been going along much better ever since.

Although it took a while for Jerry to get up the courage to confront his sponsor, he didn't just sit passively, nursing his frustrations and letting valuable time slip by. After analyzing the situation, he realized that a big part of the problem was his chair's lack of familiarity with statistical techniques. He wisely decided only a direct approach could release him from the limbo in which he found himself. Belatedly, he also began to do what he should have been doing all along, taking brief notes of each meeting. Without revealing his opinion about his advisor's inexperience in statistics, he set the stage for the advisor to realize it himself. If Jerry was resentful, he didn't show it. He let his chair save face, earned his respect by confronting him, and actually improved the quality of the relationship. In short, Jerry became "street smart."

FROM STUDENT TO SCHOLAR: A METAMORPHOSIS

You already know a good deal about the academic community you are getting ready to enter. Much of what engages you right now as a doctoral candidate will continue to engage you if you become a faculty member: developing research ideas, gathering and "massaging" data, interpreting results, and writing the research report. The difference is that as a faculty member you will have to balance research with other responsibilities such as teaching, student advising, and committee assignments.

One would have to go back to pre-World War II days to find a university environment in which teaching was valued in equal measure with research, despite lip service to the contrary. Student activism in the '60s changed the university in many ways but did little to correct the balance between these two equally vital aspects to higher education.

In the early '80s, Clark Kerr, then president of the University of California at Berkeley, observed that the focus upon research had given rise to the veneration of the non-teacher; the higher a professor's standing, the less he or she has to do with students! This trend has continued almost unabated, particularly at four-year doctorate-granting universities. A decade later, others are insisting that being a teacher should be the most prestigious post on campus, and the most highly paid. Anderson in his *Impostors in the Temple*, writes a scathing attack on today's universities saying that most research is irrelevant, lacking in substance and self-serving. More important, it deprives students of what they are entitled to, the attention of dedicated teachers who see instruction as their primary mission.[2]

"The enemy of good teaching is not research, but rather the spirit that says that this is the only worthy or legitimate task for faculty members," concludes a 1985 report of the Association of American Colleges (cited in Larry Spence, On the "Profusion of Research Publications," in Penn State online, 2001). Some of the harshest critics of the "publish or perish" philosophy come from faculty. It is a well-recognized truism that if one wants to publish, the safest route is to pick an unimportant problem, avoid challenging existing beliefs, and use simple easily understood methodology. This advice has implications for the graduate student writing a dissertation. Much as I might like to suggest that you test existing dogma and contribute something new to the field, I know the climate at universities today, and writing as a *student advocate*, I am forced to say, "pick a safe, non-controversial topic at this stage of your career." Later, as a tenured full professor, you can break new ground. The idea in writing a dissertation is simply to demonstrate your ability to conduct research. Think of it as an exercise. It is not that students don't count. They do, especially in private institutions where tuition and alumni donations help offset the cost of operation. Poor student evaluations have caused several of my colleagues to be denied tenure, in both public and private institutions.

Even in these cases, however, I believe that a distinguished publication record would have offset poor student ratings, while I seriously doubt that the reverse would be true. Good teaching "only" enhances the prof's reputation with a few students, while good research enhances the national, perhaps international, reputation of the researcher and the institution. Fortified by the knowledge that there are almost no formal penalties for bad teaching once hired, many potentially good teachers neglect this part of their work.

Obviously, publications are easier to measure than teaching ability. They can be counted, but teaching ability cannot be measured by counting anything, certainly not graduate students. Actually, the more popular the teacher, the more likely he or she will be suspected of that unpardonable sin, *coddling*. I've known of instances where junior faculty have been warned against acquiring the reputation of being a top-notch teacher or, even worse, a student advocate.

Only "full bulls" are free of the publish-or-perish criterion and even they are considered "dinosaurs" unless they publish an empirical study, a speculative article, or a philosophical treatise occasionally. A full bull, as you may already know, is a tenured professor at top academic rank.*

Although posed as opposites, good teaching and good research can be mutually supportive and enhancing. They both strive to explain, understand, and predict phenomena, and, ideally, they both employ self-correcting mechanisms against faulty reasoning.

---

*In case you're wondering, the feminine equivalent of full bull is not full cow but it clearly reflects the notion than most high-ranking academics are male.

STRAWS IN THE WIND:
A RENEWED INTEREST IN TEACHING?

Although no sustained or robust trend appears on the horizon, a few highly respected voices have been raised in support of the importance of university teaching. Stanford President Donald Kennedy chided his faculty for stressing scholarly work (read research) over teaching, and vowed to change the tenure system to give greater weight to teaching and less to research. Similarly, the University of California has increased teaching demands as part of the criteria for promotion, and the National Endowment for the Humanities and the Carnegie Foundation cited the need for a renewal of commitment to the classroom.

Despite these straws in the wind, a more equitable balance between teaching and research will not come easily. Even if the reward system changes overnight, which is highly unlikely, it will take years for deeply entrenched attitudes to change.[3] If, as a part of the professorate, you are committed to this cause, your work is cut out for you. In the meantime, prepare yourself for the status quo.

GRANT-GETTING

Another fact of professorial life you should be aware of is the need to "buy" your way out of assigned classes to make time for research. A colleague wasn't far wrong when he observed, "It's hard to get paper clips around here, much less support for research, unless you are a good grant-getter." Released time from teaching can be as short as a three unit chunk of time or as long as full-time appointment for a quarter, semester, or an academic year or more. Grant-writing is both a highly technical skill and a fine art. It requires mastery of a discipline and a knack for asking the right questions, ones that will catch the eye of a funding agency.

Grant-writing is seldom taught directly in graduate school. Whatever you may know about coaxing money from bureaucracies has probably come through working with a P.I. (principal investigator), as a research assistant, after the grant has been funded—not during it's development. It is not unrelated to previous familiar academic activities but does require a special kind of entrepreneurial talent. If you can develop grant-writing proficiency as a student you will have faculty vying for your services while, at the same time, you will be building a solid base for your own future research opportunities.

WHAT GRADUATES WISHED THEY HAD KNOWN FROM THE START

Although the primary reason for writing this book was to view the experience from the students' perspective, I also wanted a longer view tempered by whatever wisdom might be offered by newly minted Ph.D.s and professors who have been around a while. So I posed the question, "What do you know now that you wished you'd known when you entered your doctoral program?" and got the following bits of advice.

1. **Do Not Enter Doctoral Study Empty-Handed.** A surprising number of entering doctoral students still expect to be told what to do. I have news for you, they don't *give* you the doctoral degree, *you have to take it away from them!* Take the initiative in approaching faculty and present yourself as a thinker, someone full of ideas and eager to test them.

Use your time while driving, jogging, running errands, and engaging in other "no brainer" activities to mull over interesting questions and ways in which they might be approached. Begin to hone in on potential research problems early in your course work and determine for yourself why some ideas appeal and others do not.

2. **Expect to "Sell Yourself" to Your Sponsor.** Since no faculty member is obligated to sponsor any particular student, the way you present yourself is important. Faculty are naturally attracted to bright students at all levels of education and this is especially true at the doctoral level where profs' own careers are directly influenced by the caliber of their students. In fact, it is not unusual for faculty to vie among themselves to sponsor an especially bright student, although this fact seldom leaks out of faculty circles.

3. **Don't Worry About the Possibility of Change in Focus.** Having some fairly solid initial views about your dissertation topic won't bind you irrevocably, nor will it matter if you are slightly wide

of what turns out to be the final target. What does matter is that you have begun to think like a researcher and to present yourself as one. Even if the final topic has little resemblance to the original, the time spent putting it together will be more of an investment than a loss.

4. **Realize the Importance of Self-Management.** It is absolutely vital to keep a firm hand on the process of moving through, around, and over the various hurdles of doctoral study. Within the seven-year limit that most universities impose, the pace you set is pretty much self-determined. All your student life you have been accustomed to having deadlines imposed upon you; now you must impose deadlines on yourself.

A sense of control will grow out of your realization that you are making steady and substantial progress toward your goal, and the reverse is equally true. Your pace will vary. There will be times when things click into place and times when everything seems to go wrong. The important thing to remember is that the answer to whatever quandary you find yourself in at the moment is just around the corner, so hang in there. The firmer conceptual grasp you have of your project and the more disciplined you are in pursuit of it, the more in control you will be.

Consider the plight of Al, who had been advanced to candidacy six months before I spoke with him. He knew in a general way the inquiry he wanted to make but couldn't get faculty agreement on how to do it. He was stalled at the point of writing the dissertation proposal.

> Each member of my committee that I talk with has a different notion about what variables I should use and how I should go about measuring them. I was so happy to find three faculty who were interested in my idea of doing an ethnographic study of life in a retirement community. But now one says I need to take a course in qualitative measurement and another says I'd better do more reading on the dynamics of aging. I feel like I'm getting the run-around and I'll never get this proposal written at this rate.

In his enthusiasm, Al presented his ideas prematurely before he had the main building blocks of his research clearly in mind. In doing so, he tarnished his good first impression and left faculty thinking he was indecisive, therefore not ready for the next step. A professor who had been interested in the topic commented that she didn't intend to write the dissertation for him and it looked like that was the kind of help he was going to need.[4]

SUMMARY

Those who seek Ph.D.s in the social sciences, humanities, and most professional schools, must undergo the difficult metamorphosis from student to scholar in a largely indifferent, laissez-faire environment. It is easier to find faculty advisors than mentors.

As a social scientist interested in human attitudes and behaviors, you work with "soft" data which require some of the most sophisticated statistical techniques employed in research. Few students have had enough experience to handle empirical research at this level without expert help so get help if you need it. You don't have to be a genius to get a Ph.D. You do have to be reasonably intelligent, but then other traits take over. Psychologically, one of the big challenges is to cope with the double messages, being treated as a colleague one day and a "go-fer" the next. Your success depends in no small measure on your ability to establish good relationships with faculty and this calls for just the right mixture of humility and assertiveness. On the whole, however, assertive students do better than too timid or passive ones. Doctoral pursuit is not for the faint-hearted. Mastering contradictory roles is particularly difficult for those who have held positions of responsibility out there in the "real world."

Changes usually do not come rapidly in large institutions, yet by the time readers of this book are faculty members, the critics of the current practice of emphasizing research over teaching may have had an effect. As important as I believe they both are, there is little doubt that professors are rewarded primarily for their research and not for their teaching skills; this has implications for all levels of teaching. However, there is some evidence that this is changing.

NOTES

1. Parsons quotes one university press publisher who maintains that dissertation writers are brow-beaten by their committees into writing something unpublishable and it is difficult to turn this "dissertationese" back into "humanese." If you are

interested in converting your dissertation to a book, I highly recommend Parsons. P.: *Getting Published: The Acquisition Process at University Presses.* Knoxville, The University of Tennessee Press, 1989.

2. Martin Anderson. formerly a professor and currently a senior fellow at the Hoover Institution at Stanford University, attacks many traditional academic practices. In addition to condemning the use of graduate students as teachers and the trivial nature of most research, he observes that the typical graduate student is in no position to complain to anyone about anything. There is simply too much pressure to put the professor's interests before the interests of the student. See Anderson, Martin: *Impostors in the Temple.* New York, Simon & Schuster, 1992.

3. Particularly in large public universities, students are at the bottom of the picking order and professors are trapped in a vicious cycle of chasing research grants and publishing research reports. Academics and the public are increasingly more critical of institutions which attempt to attract nationally known scholars by promising them light teaching loads or no teaching responsibilities at all. San Francisco Chronicle, April 6, 1990 and *San Diego Union*, March 19, 1991 and *The Los Angeles Times*, San Diego edition, July 17, 1992.

4. See Sternberg, David: *How to Complete and Survive a Doctoral Dissertation.* New York, St. Martin's Press, 1992.

Chapter 3

CHOOSING A DISSERTATION TOPIC

Two "ABDs" were waiting for an elevator at a conference in downtown Chicago. Former classmates, they recognized each other at the same moment.

Hi Gerald, how are you coming with your dissertation?

I still haven't settled on a topic, I'm embarrassed to tell you. Adolescent development is such a big field. First I looked at teenage parenthood, then at unwed mothers, and now I'm interested in dropout patterns in inner city schools. Nothing seems just right. My wife is giving me a bad time-she says I'm turning into a professional student! Why can finding a dissertation topic be so difficult?

You are surrounded by ideas, many of which would make an interesting topic. Ideas leap from the printed page, they fall like pearls from the lips of speakers, and a few are even exciting enough to awaken you in the middle of the night. In retrospect, when you finally put those long-sought-after words together, it all seems so simple. "The Effects of Relocation upon the Disabled Elderly," "Mother-Infant Interaction and Language Development," or "The Role of Compassion in Ralph Waldo Emerson's Writings: 1841 to 1844." What could be more straightforward?

Yet the process of carving out a topic from among what seems to be an infinite number of possibilities is anything but simple. Usually it is the result of months of vigorous intellectual effort and considerable emotional investment. Perhaps the problem is the realization that this innocent-sounding title will have the power to dominate most of your waking hours for several years to come.

DOZENS OF "RIGHT" TOPICS

Very few enter doctoral study knowing exactly what they want to investigate, and most agonize unnecessarily over finding just the right topic. This is misdirected energy. Within your field of study there are probably dozens of topics which will facilitate your quest. It is a bit like marriage; there is probably more than one person on the face of the earth with whom a satisfactory life could be built. What makes the choice succeed or fail depends mostly on what you do about it after the choice has been made.

THE PURPOSE OF A DISSERTATION

Let us start by being clear about the reason for writing a dissertation in the first place. Although the *manner* in which this purpose is fulfilled varies enormously, depending upon the requirements of the particular sponsor or department, there is really only one reason for writing a dissertation and that is to demonstrate your ability to conduct research.

Some will tell you that the way to do this is to design a project that will make an *original* and *significant* contribution to the field of inquiry. No matter how often these traditional words are spoken however, the truth is that most dissertations make an original contribution, but few make a significant (in the sense of profound) contribution to the theory, practice or policy-making of their disciplines.

Unfortunately, thousands of students have been burdened with the idea that nothing short of a *magnum opus* will do. They waste months and years trying to achieve the impossible, or at least the impractical. Now is not the ideal time, nor is the dissertation the ideal vehicle, to produce a deathless *tome*. Realize at the outset that your dissertation is unlikely to make your name a household word or to shake the foundations of your discipline. View it as an exercise in scholarship that will make a modest contribution to the body of knowledge and be an asset in your search for a faculty position if that is your goal. A dissertation that is well chosen and executed can also be a gold mine of researchable questions for future investigations. From modest beginnings, some scholars spend years developing and refining their original topics and eventually become recognized authorities in the subject matter of their dissertations.

Wrong Reasons for Doctoral Pursuit

At the beginning of your search for a topic, and before you invest time and energy in pursuit of a Ph.D., let me mention a couple of typical, but wrong-headed, reasons for seeking this degree.

To Proselytize a Cherished Cause. Researchers differ from missionaries, reformers, and most laypersons in the way they are taught to approach problems. Being convinced of the answer before you even ask the question is antithetical to the tenets of scientific inquiry, and such attitudes greatly undermine your credibility. Down the road, your research efforts may indeed lead to righting social, political, or economic wrongs but these are inappropriate goals for the research itself. Only well-designed empirical tests can answer questions posed in your dissertation.

Because Everyone Expects You To. I have known students who did well through the preliminaries but were miserable at the dissertation stage. Despite their anguish they plowed doggedly on, too embarrassed to admit even to themselves that this topic was not for them. Don't quit at the first sign of difficulty, but if, after diligent soul-searching, you conclude that the game is not worth the candle, cut your losses and get out. You will survive the initial embarrassment and be better off for facing the truth early on instead of investing time in a venture for which you have little aptitude or appetite.

The only reason I can think of to undergo this formidable task is that you find your broad field of inquiry so intrinsically interesting that you want to spend a lifetime exploring it, teaching it, and writing about it. If this sounds appealing, you will probably be a happy laborer in the academic vineyards of your specialty for a lifetime.

WHEN TO LOOK FOR A TOPIC

In education as in many of the social sciences it is customary to have the student select the research problem to be investigated. Then it becomes the student's responsibility to find a professor who is interested enough in the project and confident enough in the student's ability to sponsor the work.

In the sciences, research topics are typically assigned to conform to the advisor's research interests and projects. Some investigations may even be conducted for a commercial enterprise outside academe. In such cases, the student doesn't have much choice—the project is already well-defined and he or she fits into the existing structure.

There are advantages both ways. Having the path well-marked and led by an advisor engaged in an established project has obvious benefits. On the other hand it is exhilarating to have the freedom to follow one's own hunches and pursue one's own goals.

A colleague of mine with a deaf child knew what he wanted to research long before he was admitted to candidacy. He had an obvious personal as well a scholarly interest in deaf education. His early commitment gave him a head start, because he already knew a lot about the subject and where he wanted to focus. He could select courses with this disability in mind and occasionally shape class assignments to fit his interests. He wrote a dissertation on the quality of relationships between deaf individuals and those with normal hearing. It was an area not well-researched and one of the few dissertations that has made an impact on education.

If you are able to pursue your own research topic, the earlier you select one the better, but there is one caveat. You do run the risk of foreclosing more promising topics as you explore the subject. Even if this happens, those intriguing questions will be waiting for you after you have earned your degree.

The following section is predicated on the assumption that you are free to work on a topic of your choice.

WHERE TO LOOK FOR A TOPIC

Whether you start from scratch or have a project well in mind, your journey begins with a search of the literature. Without a thorough knowledge of what has gone before, you cannot determine your own path. You need to immerse yourself in the ideas, conclusions and inferences drawn by other researchers. Look for gaps in the body of knowledge and errors of omission as well as commission. Work from the general to the specific by starting with generic ideas that fall within the ballpark of your interests and gradually narrow the field.

Reading copies of dissertations accepted in your department will give you a sense of the kind of investigations that have been supported. It will also tell you who on the faculty have served as sponsors and committee members in that realm of inquiry. Look at the conclusions and suggestions for further research. Authors often indicate findings in need of clarification and cite promising new avenues to explore. Without an inordinate amount of time reading other people's dissertations, you will quickly develop an appreciation of good writing and sensitize yourself to jargon and wordiness.

Professional Journals

Probably the best sources for dissertation ideas are to be found in the professional journals in your own and in closely-related fields. Such journals also contain the most recent findings, despite the one to four years in turnaround time it takes from submission to publication. Look for seminal studies that have shaped the direction of research over time as well as for those on the cutting edge. These will help you bracket your own work.

As you read, try to determine the theoretical constructs underlying each inquiry and ask yourself how this study supports or refutes its theoretical underpinnings. What unresolved controversies are still provocative in the area? Do you see holes in the current findings that need to be plugged? Maybe there are sub-groups of people who have been ignored because no one thought to test them or because it was assumed that no significant differences would be found between them and the mainstream population. These are the kinds of assumptions it might be profitable to question.

SOURCES

The problem is generally an overabundance of data, not insufficient information. The following is a short list of possible sources which have links to other sites.

American Educational Research Association (AERA)–promotes educational research and its practical applications.

Higher Education Research Institute (HERI)–Information Studies – Home of the CIRP – The nation's oldest and largest study of higher education.

Internet Scout Project–Home of the Scout Report, the Internet's longest-running weekly publication.

ERIC Clearinghouse for social studies/social science education - National Library of Education.

Social Science Electronic Publishing: Social Science Research Network-SSRN is devoted to a rapid worldwide dissemination of social science research and is composed of numbers of specialized research networks in each of the social sciences.

Social Sciences and Humanities Research Council–Federal funding agency for university-based research and graduate training in the social sciences and humanities.

The Center for the Humanities–Fellowship; Internet Scout Project-Home of the Scout Report, the Internet's longest research and writing, supporting individual research and teaching.

Modern Humanities Research Association (MHRA)–Home page. Supports scholarly publishing projects.

Other Communication Systems:

Twitter: Free social networking and micro-blogging
Chat rooms: A way to keep in touch with professors and colleagues.
Blogs: Use this as a kind of diary, a collection of links for your private thoughts or memos to the world.
Skype: allows you to make free and low-cost video and voice calls internationally.

Seminars, Discussions, and Conferences

Lectures, class discussions, and informal dialogues provide fertile ground for ferreting out dissertation topics. Keep your ears open during class discussions and capitalize on verbal interchanges. Enter dialogues with professors and fellow students. Play devil's advocate with other peoples ideas: challenge their theoretical assumptions, question the appropriateness of their methodologies, contest their choice of variables, and argue with their results. Ask for a similar examination of your own ideas. When this is done in the time-honored spirit of intellectual combat, it helps everyone sharpen their analytical and synthesizing skills and the capacity to construct logical, internally consistent arguments. Not everybody is willing to engage in such give-and-take, so you have to be selective. Fellow students are your best bet.

For up-to-the-minute information on cutting-edge topics, it is hard to beat programs at conferences. Try to get a copy of the program and write presenters for papers in those sessions that are in your "ballpark."

Student Discussion Groups

Many departments and some graduate divisions have doctoral student associations. If yours does not, I strongly advise you to form one, the more informal the better. You don't need dues, officers, attendance records, or by-laws. All you need to do is to bring a few doctoral students together for a brown bag lunch or a "TGIF" at the commons or someone's home. The purpose is to encourage lively debate and to facilitate the exchange of ideas on a regular basis. While these groups are usually comprised of students from the same academic department, don't overlook the outsider who might enrich the discussion by adding a new dimension.

Worried about someone stealing your topic? I have never known this to happen. Announcing one's topic in a public forum seems to establish a kind of informal copyright—more a protection than a danger. Moreover, a single topic can yield a huge variety of studies without encroaching upon another investigation. Don't panic if you hear that someone else is working upon "your" topic and by the same reasoning, don't claim that you are the first ever to address this issue—professors are amused or annoyed at such naiveté. Nine times out of ten, someone, somewhere, some time, has tackled it, albeit in a slightly different way.

Although the doctoral candidates with whom I worked used their peer group in this way, they also found it valuable for conducting practice sessions in preparation for the oral defense. Interestingly, students are nearly always tougher and more searching in their questioning than professors, so when the real thing comes along, it is almost anti-climactic. Having survived the student "inquisition," most candidates go to their orals well prepared, both intellectually and emotionally. The practice sessions are nearly always mutually beneficial, with questioners learning as much as the questioned.

Resisting the Seductiveness of Research

There seems to be something very seductive about the business of searching the literature, tracking down documents, and recording information. Students tend to get hung up at this stage, lulled into a false sense of accomplishment while moving no closer to the goal. Eventually, the perusal of other peoples' research must give way to the formidable task of beginning your own.

A good way to counteract this tendency to escape from reality is to force yourself to write a research question (or statement) daily about a promising topic. It doesn't matter whether it is related to that particular day's reading or is a variation of a research question you wrote a week ago. Forcing yourself to move from the abstract to the concrete makes the next step, that of implementation, much easier and there is no substitute for the discipline of writing the essence of the investigation in one concise sentence. Date each new or revised statement and add it to the others, keeping the entire list handy for future reference.

Topic Seeking Strategies

Over the years, I have observed three distinct patterns of topic-seeking behaviors. The first two are not so much strategies as shotgun approaches. I have labeled each one in an effort to bring into awareness what tends to be less than conscious behavior. These approaches are: the expedient approach, the procedure-first approach, and the theory-based problem-oriented approach.

1. **The Expedient Approach.** The presence of an easily available data source is a powerful motivator for this mode of attack and seems to create an almost irresistible urge to grab the data while they're "hot." Such motivation is understandable because data sources have the unfortunate tendency to evaporate into thin air. Willing participants turn unwilling or scatter to the ends of the earth when the researcher hesitates too long. Human subjects are more difficult to obtain than guinea pigs or chemicals. School children, previously the guinea pigs of education research, are fiercely protected today because of research, showing the strong relationship between time-on-task and academic achievement. Educators don't want school children diverted from their daily lessons. Safeguarding all human (and animal) subjects is important and necessary, yet it does increase the difficulties in securing subjects and the temptation to grab the first subject pool available.

The disadvantages of the expediency model are illustrated in the case of Gary, a former student of mine who was accepted into a Ph.D. program in clinical psychology at a nearby university. I found him late one afternoon waiting dejectedly in the hall by my office. Unlocking my door and motioning him to a chair, I asked him what was wrong. That opened a floodgate.

> Talk about Catch-22! My advisor doesn't like my sample and I have already agreed to test kids at a youth club in a low-income part of town where my wife is a social worker.
>
> I figured these kids would exhibit some emotional problems that I could use as independent variables. Well, I just finished a battery of tests and—guess what—they turned out to be as normal as apple pie!
>
> Now my advisor is mad at me for not doing a pilot study first. She wants me to start all over again with a different group. I can't do that because my wife's boss is expecting the results of my study and I've gotta deliver. Six months work is down the drain and I've just about decided to quit torturing myself and get the hell out of here!

Using our perfect 20-20 hindsight, Gary and I identified three of his most glaring errors. He had picked the wrong group out of expediency, he had operated on a stereotype instead of conducting a pilot test, and (the biggest mistake of all) he had endangered his relationship with his advisor because he was in too much of a hurry to follow her suggestions. Gary's academic career, not to mention his sanity, were saved when we were able to match the first group with a second group of adolescents similar in all important respects except that they attended a continuation school and had histories of academic and emotional problems. Mending his fences with his advisor took a while, but he wisely refrained from any mention of me or of his determination to placate his wife's boss!

Despite an inauspicious beginning, Gary's proposal was eventually well-received by his committee and he was awarded the degree two years later. Although he ultimately reached his goal, he had to work backward by contriving a problem that fit his sample, instead of the other way around.

2. The Procedure-First Approach. As with the expediency model, the procedure-first approach forces the researcher to work backward, from the methodology to the research problem itself. This kind of thing happens when the researcher falls in love with a procedure and then sets about finding ways to employ it. No matter how fascinated you might be with the power of the Mann-Whitney U Test or how intrigued you are with the elegance of Stephenson's Q Sort technique, don't let the methodology drive the problem. Keep the horse in front of the cart where it belongs by determining the problem first and then designing methodology to fit it.

3. The Theory-Based/Problem-Oriented Approach. Now we come to the preferred strategy where the investigation is firmly anchored in theory and the problem drives methodology instead of the other way around. What is so important about theory? A former professor of mine used to say that all researchers use theory but they just differ in the degree to which they were *aware* of the theory they use. A good theory is a highly practical tool in the hands of a competent researcher. It is a set of interrelated constructs (concepts), definitions, and propositions that presents a systematic view of phenomena by specifying relations among variables, with the purpose of explaining and predicting the phenomena.[1]

Theories are used to test, understand, and explain patterns (relations among variables) instead of trying to explain each separate event in isolation. We are not looking for the capital "T" kind of truth of course, but rather for a set of assumptions which are valid for the circumstances in which we plan to apply the theory. We assume the theory to be true, at least temporarily, for the purpose of following some course of action.

Because of the technicalities of theory-building, some dissertation chairs suggest you base your research upon already-established theories or parts of theories, since testing an entire theory is usually too ambitious an undertaking for a single dissertation. Using an already established, widely used theory makes it unnecessary to justify the theory itself, only its *relevance for your inquiry.*

You may, however, decide to build your own theoretical framework in order to impose structure and order upon the information, the hunches, and the insights that you have collected about your problem. If you go this route, I advise constructing a flowchart which describes the interrelationships of the various parts and may be used as a map to guide the process. Keep it simple and straightforward if you plan to complete your degree sometime before the onset of the next ice age.

Whatever course you take, theoretical underpinnings will provide the context for your study and enable you to explain its rationale and relevance. If you fail to face up to the issue of theory at the beginning of your project, it may rise to haunt you at your final orals when an examiner asks, "Now that you have found people tend to behave this way under these conditions, how does this outcome affect your initial theoretical position?"

CRITERIA FOR CHOOSING A TOPIC

You now have a cornucopia of promising ideas in retrievable form together with some sense of the theoretical implications of each one. It is time to assess the feasibility of each potential topic by some criteria. The following list of questions may prove helpful in this task.

1. Is it Manageable? This is the first question to ask yourself because of the tendency of beginning researchers to select unwieldy topics. Are you doing a biographic study of an historic or literary figure? Instead of attempting to cover Wordsworth's entire life, you might focus upon that eventful year, 1797–1798, in which his friendship with Coleridge flourished and he was inspired to write the famous Lyrical Ballads.

Strive to develop a tightly reasoned (simple but elegant) investigation with a view toward feasibility. Ask, "Do I have the resources (persons, information, time) to do this? Does it advance my career plans?"

2. Is it Within the Range of my Competence? Some aspects of your proposed topic may require you to digress for the purpose of acquiring new skills. The struggle to gain sufficient mastery of statistics to carry out an empirical investigation might be enough of a challenge without trying to grasp an entirely new field or technique. Deafness, for example, is a complex disability and a researcher needs to understand the physical, emotional, and social implications of deafness to judge its behavioral implications.

A documentary study requires ability to use specialized research techniques pertinent to the particular source: archival data (census information), personal or private data (life histories, diaries, confessions, secret files), and public data (mass media, literature). In addition to unique skills needed to manage specialized areas, all topics require a degree of literary proficiency.

3. Is the Data Source Reliable? Make certain that data for your topic will be available some months down the line when you reach the data-gathering stage. Access to records can fluctuate with changes in personnel and interview arrangements made in good faith can disappear over night as Jill learned the hard way.

> I jumped at the chance when Professor N offered to let me use his data base in exchange for my statistical help on his project. Sure, I knew he didn't have tenure here but I thought if I helped him publish, it would clinch a position for him and help me at the same time.
>
> I was really blown away when I came to work one morning and found he had accepted a tenure-track position at another institution. He didn't even have the guts to face me . . . just took off with his grant and his data leaving me high and dry!

Fortunately, this doesn't happen often, as most professors are more ethical than Jill's, but the fact that it happens at all is enough to make you wary of contractual arrangements with non-tenured professors. Rising stars, tenured or not, can be good bets to hitch your wagon to, but finding out whether they are going to be awarded tenure isn't always easy. Although faculty rosters showing *current* academic rank are easily available, it is the *future* status of a prof with whom you seek to establish a relationship that has a direct bearing upon your own future. Dependence upon a non-tenured person is risky unless the signs are strong that he or she is to become a permanent member of the department. All I can say is, "When in doubt, don't."

4. Does it Make a Significant and Original Contribution? The criterion of significance was discussed at the beginning of the chapter where we noted that "significant" here doesn't mean "profound." When your topic is approved, you can assume that it is significant enough to make a modest contribution to your field of inquiry. Its long-range affect on the discipline will depend upon your skill as a researcher as well as its timing in the marketplace of ideas. Don't worry about the timing (so much of it is pure luck) just concentrate on developing the skills to do a respectable job.

Now what about the other criterion, "original?" Unless you plagiarize, your work will be original. It will be written in your own words even though your ideas will certainly have emerged in some form from a wide variety of sources. Sequences of words can be protected by copyright, and usually are, but ideas are more nebulous, harder to trace. Credit is due the author of an idea when you know the source, yet no matter how careful you are it is impossible to trace every idea to its beginnings.

5. Is it Controversial? This raises a delicate and troubling issue in an environment which ostensibly promotes free speech and claims to champion the pursuit of truth wherever it may lead. Unhappily, "groupthink" operates within the academy as well as outside of it, and the system needs people who will refuse to blindly echo the party line. Moreover, one of the marks of good research is its penchant for controversy, its stimulus of debate, and its power to challenge intellectual boundaries.

Despite my strong convictions about the freedom (even the obligation) to dissent, I am writing this book as a *student advocate.* Therefore, my advice is to wait until you have all the trappings of academic rank the Ph.D., a position, and tenure, before undertaking extremely controversial or unpopular topics.

Even then it is not an activity for the timid or thin-skinned! One well-established researcher and geneticist, Arthur Jensen, became *persona non grata* on campuses across this nation after publishing findings suggesting a genetically-based difference in IQ between blacks and whites.[2] Even more pertinent to this discussion, a journalism *student* studying contemporary sex roles in Saudi Arabia became the target of an extremely vicious attack from the Saudis and some NATO countries in 1980 for his dissertation film, "Death of A Princess."

Pursuit of the doctorate is fraught with enough difficulties without deliberately taking on powerful opposition groups. Having said that, I trust that conservatism won't become habitual, stifling your healthy inclinations to question prevailing opinion.

6. Is it Interesting to Me? For the immediate future, you are going to live with this topic to a degree you would have never before thought possible. It will claim precious time usually spent with loved ones and it will supersede almost all of the activities you used to consider essential to the quality of life. Anything short of this kind of interest and single-minded commitment will be insufficient to get the job done. Even the most dedicated scholars will occasionally feel like Sisyphus, sentenced by Zeus to forever push a rock up a hill only to have it roll back down upon his head. The more engrossing the topic, the better able you will be to overcome the inevitable frustrations and obstacles along the way. A choice wisely made and competently executed is an investment in your future; dissertation topics have a way of turning into professional specialties.

Avoid Broad and Unwieldy Topics

After selecting the general subject matter of your dissertation, you are ready to translate this idea into a project, something sufficiently circumscribed to be finished in a single lifetime. Consider these three overly-broad and unwieldy topics: (1) "Theories of Education," (2) "Protecting the Environment," and (3) "The Classical Humanists."

Now let us sharpen the focus of these three titles so that they become more manageable: (1) "Thomas Dewey's Reflective Theory and Concept Formation among Gifted Fourth Graders"; (2) "'Natural Burn Policies and the Management of Our National Park System: Yellowstone, a Case in Point"; and (3) "Classical Humanistic Values and the Reality of Anti-Semitism in the United States in the 1980s."

As revised, these titles have greatly reduced the scope of the investigative fields in all three instances. In the first case, instead of trying to cover all of the theories on education, a single aspect of one well-known theorist's position is examined using an identified human subject group. In the second case, an extremely controversial environmental issue is studied within the context of the Yellowstone fire of 1989. In the third case, a current social issue is framed within a ten-year span and examined through an ancient lens.

Researchable Ideas

- The Relationship Between Homelessness and Susceptibility to Drugs
- Birth Order and Success in Sixth Grade Classes
- Acceptance of Gays in College
- Success Strategies for Women and People of Color
- Is Affirmative Action Passé?
- Is There Less Apraxia in Asian Language Speakers?
- Subtle Discrimination and its Effects in a Private School Environment.
- The Role of Mentoring for Those Seeking the Ph.D. Psychology in San Diego State University.
- Depression, Causes and Cures` as Related to Birth Order.

THE PROBLEM STATEMENT

Some faculty recommend that you delay writing the problem statement or research question until you find a sponsor. It is true that the problem statement you write initially may very well be modified, even discarded, after consultation with your dissertation director. Nevertheless, I think presenting a well-formulated problem statement to a potential sponsor indicates that you have a grasp of what research is all about and argues strongly in your favor.

In simplest terms, a problem statement is an inquiry about the relationship between two or more variables. Whether it is a statement or a question, it explains succinctly what you plan to do. Instead of, "Are children of working mothers any worse off than those of mothers who stay at home?" ask, "Are children whose mothers work outside the home more self-sufficient (or aggressive, or productive, or socially-oriented) than children of mothers who do not?" The key abstractions, "working" and "self-sufficiency," as well as other important concepts, must be represented by empirical terms (variables) so they can be observed and measured. Does *working* mean eight hours of paid outside employment per day? How is *self-sufficiency* defined and what instruments will be used to measure it?

What evidence, in the form of research outcomes, will you accept as an affirmative answer to your research question? Of course, you do not expect to answer the research question with a simple "yes" or "no," but rather to make a number of probabilistic statements about the extent to which a relationship among variables does or does not exist.

ASSUMPTIONS

The research question or problem statement arises out of assumptions that are part of the theoretical position you use. Assumptions are not subject to verification but are accepted as theoretical constructs describing the circumstances where the theory is applicable. An illustration may help.

Leadership is a construct commonly used in politics, business, education, and informal social situations. For many years, leadership was assumed to be a trait which resided within the person and was relatively constant across settings and circumstances. Leaders would act like leaders no matter who the followers were or what the circumstances happened to be.

This theoretical assumption was later challenged by another which held that leadership is more of a *behavior* than a *trait*, and is strongly influenced by the attitudes and activities of followers as well as by the nature of the task. This could explain why a domineering boss on the job could turn into a Mr. Milquetoast at home, or why a person could step into leadership in a crisis situation but remain a follower under most circumstances. Research based upon this more complex theory of leadership behavior would not have the luxury of referring to "natural leaders." It would have to take under consideration numerous other variables and subject the data to much more sophisticated statistical analysis. Under the leadership-as-a-trait theory, where personal characteristics are thought to be relatively consistent and independent of the environment, the Jekyll and Hydes of this world would be extremely difficult to explain.

SUMMARY

The purpose of a dissertation is to demonstrate your ability to conduct research, with a minimum of faculty input. It isn't to create a *magnum opus*, or change the course of your discipline. While the choice should not be made nonchalantly, most students waste valuable time searching for exactly the right topic.

Seminars, conferences, study groups and informal discussions can suggest research ideas and strategies. Ask yourself if the topic you are considering is manageable and within your range of competence. Make sure your data source will be there when you need it and avoid extremely controversial and unwieldy topics. Your initial attempt to write a problem statement on the subject will give you an idea about the topic's feasibility. Finally, make sure you understand the assumptions and theory underlying your problem, they are critical to everything you do, from your research design to your interpretation of findings.

NOTES

1. Kerlinger takes a strong position in regard to the importance of theory-based research, describing theory as the most basic aim of science. See Kerlinger, Fred N.: *Foundations of Behavioral Research.* New York: Holt. Rinehart and Winston, 1964, p. 11
2. Jensen. Arthur R.: *Educability and Group Differences*, New York: Harper & Row, 1973. Despite a distinguished career in academe, Jensen's findings on black/white differences not only made him unwelcome on college campuses but publishers were reluctant, even afraid, to put his work into print.

Chapter 4

YOUR CHAIR, YOUR COMMITTEE, AND YOU

Esther wipes away drops of perspiration collecting on her forehead and faces her interrogator uncertainly. Fighting panic, she thinks, "Things have been going so well up to now . . . but I should have known that ol' boy would ask me the most esoteric question he could think of. Let's see now, what *was* the statistical reasoning for that analysis?"

Catching the eye of her dissertation chair, she remembers that they covered this point during a recent practice run of the oral defense. Her memory jogged, she looks the "ol' boy" squarely in the eye, rephrases his question and manages to construct a reasonably cogent answer.

This little scene illustrates a very important point, the single most important relationship you will ever make as a doctoral student is the one with your dissertation chair.[1]

It was the morning after the Big Event, and Esther and I were conducting the usual "post mortem" about her experience.

> I knew perfectly well the statistical reasoning behind that method, but when Dr. X asked his question that oblique way, my mind went blank. Then I remembered my chair said when a question was confusing, I should try to rephrase it in order to make sure I understood-to give myself a little more time to think. Hey, it worked! I am now a Ph.D.!

Esther's initial panicky reaction to Dr. X's question was caused partly by his awkward wording of the question and partly by his well-

---

1 The terms, chair, sponsor, advisor, and thesis director are used synonymously, while *mentor* is reserved for someone with long-term commitment to a student's professional and personal growth.

deserved reputation for being a fierce interrogator. She was intellectually and emotionally prepared to defend her thesis, so a reassuring glance from her chair was enough to help her regain her composure. Despite their near-collegial relationship, however, there were times when Esther felt her chair was excessively demanding. Looking back, she realized he'd put pressure on her in order to develop her self- confidence, rather than diminish it. Between them, they had identified and compensated for weaknesses in her background. A shaky preparation in math was offset by her strong conceptual grasp of statistics, and years of practical experience that helped her apply research findings to real life settings.

No Short Cuts on the Road to Understanding

Most important, Esther hadn't taken any unnecessary short cuts. Although the statistical analyses were difficult for her, she resisted the temptation to turn this responsibility over to a paid consultant. Instead, she grappled personally with each analysis, albeit with the consultant's help. Also, every written word was her own and every quote was properly cited. Going into the oral she was further buoyed by the knowledge that her mentor believed she was ready to face this final challenge. Although she had hoped to sail through the defense of the thesis without a single hitch, she was realistic enough to know that this happens only rarely and was grateful to have come through the experience successfully and as unscathed as she did.

It isn't necessary to have an *ideal* relationship with your chair in order to be successful. The majority of students, in fact, settle for much less than Esther had. One professor had this to say about the experiences of African Americans in our colleges and universities.

> My study of mentoring experiences of African Americans during their graduate and professional education revealed that only one in eight persons has ever had a true mentor, as distinguished from sponsors for specific purposes, advisers, and guides. Given the multitude of constraints imposed upon most professors, the majority of students (graduate or undergraduate) manage to traverse the academic maze without ever having a true mentoring experience.[1]

Even if your sponsor doesn't quite measure up to being a true mentor, you do need to find someone with whom you can communicate, who is knowledgeable in your area, who is politically astute, and who has enough interest in you to see you through the process. As with other significant relationships, this one flourishes at times and wanes at other times. The two of you are bound together, through thick and thin, for better or for worse, not "till death do you part" (thankfully) but at least until you get your degree. Oh yes, "divorce" is possible and this important matter will be discussed later in this chapter.

SEQUENCE OF STEPS

Prior to choosing a chair, you will be assigned an academic advisor on the basis of what appears to be a good early match between your research interests and the advisor's expertise. Your academic advisor will help you select classes in a program of study designed to facilitate your professional goals. When the classroom phase is over and you have passed qualifying exams ("quals"), sometimes called preliminary exams ("prelims"), you will be advanced to candidacy and enter the dissertation phase of your work. At this point your academic advisor will leave and a dissertation chair will take over. Occasionally, the original arrangement works so well for both parties that the academic advisor agrees to stay on as dissertation chair.

Although I have outlined these steps sequentially, some of them can, and occasionally do, take place concurrently. A few students come into doctoral study having an understanding with a potential sponsor, although this is not typical. Students usually begin to look for a dissertation chair sometime before completion of the last qual or prelim. Most have only a vague idea of either their dissertation topic or the person they want as chair until well into their sequence of classes. Although no one pattern is superior to any other, it is never too early to establish a relationship with one or more potential dissertation chairs. Professors are understandably reluctant to commit themselves to someone they scarcely know and students are well advised to share the same reservations for similar reasons.

THOSE RARE INDIVIDUALS, MENTORS

It is an exceptional dissertation chair who deserves to be called a *mentor*. Most chairs are more like advisors, not advocates, although they do a reasonably adequate job of supervising research projects and guiding their charges through the circuitous path to the Ph.D.

Mentors, in contrast to advisors, do more than simply stand and point the way. Mentors accompany their protégés throughout the entire process. This calls for a professional and emotional investment of a different order, one characterized by a strong commitment to the student as a person as well as a neophyte scholar. Mentor-protégé relationships seem to emerge somewhat mysteriously out of the chemistry between two people and out of a shared interest in the discipline. Clearly, such affiliations cannot be mandated administratively. When they do occur, they grow gradually as communication becomes easier and trust overcomes earlier doubts and periods of testing.

Growing Collegiality

At first, students defer to the authority of the mentor but as they gain in knowledge and self-confidence, they feel freer to challenge his or her point of view. Intellectual independence is usually recognized as a sign of intellectual growth and encouraged by mentors. Lively verbal exchanges are enormously valuable to the student, especially when conducted in a safe environment with a skilled and knowledgeable sparring partner. The very essence of research is, of course, asking questions, challenging established doctrines, testing theoretical premises, and contradicting the authorities. What began as a device to support the student, can grow through the years into a lasting and mutually beneficial association where power and authority are fully shared.

A particularly insightful friend of mine reminisced about the love-hate aspects of his relationship with his mentor, contrasting his early perceptions with the view he currently holds:

> I clearly remember my feelings of powerlessness and vulnerability. While I admired him from the start, I also kept saying to myself, "this man is picky, picky, picky!" Sometime in the ensuing 20 years, however, it dawned on me that I have been the beneficiary of those high demands and I realized that the times we spent together were money in the bank, intellectually speaking.
>
> In the last few years, our relationship has *literally* provided money in the bank because we have co-authored two very successful books. I have to tell you, I really love that man.

Mentor-protege relationships aren't limited to academe, of course, but occur in a variety of settings: businesses, factories, government offices, and even on Hollywood movie sets. They take on special meaning in academia however, because the roots of this relationship are buried deep in antiquity.

Prototype Mentors

A prototype mentor, you will remember, is found in the Greek epic, *Odyssey*, when Odysseus places his son in the care of a trusted guardian before starting his journey to Troy. Centuries later, a similar benevolent figure appears in the *Divine Comedy* when Virgil materializes at critical times during Dante's long and hazardous passage through the bizarre and dangerous nether regions in search of Beatrice. Virgil is the perfect mentor, knowledgeable, trustworthy, and caring. Moreover, he is a seasoned traveler, having trod that path many times before, and he interprets enigmatic signs, warns of dangers ahead, and steadies the faltering steps of his protégé. On the other hand, he is clearly no patsy. He forces Dante to develop his own resources by using just the right mix of challenge, inspiration, discipline, and support.

Outgrowing the Relationship

Good mentors, like good houseguests, know when it is time to go. When the journey is finally over and the traveler has reached her destination, the original relationship has served its purpose. It must be replaced with a different one reflecting the new Ph.D.'s altered status. Wise mentors more or less consciously make this transition with each graduate, gladly relinquishing a student in favor of gaining a colleague. Others seem to lack the ego strength to surrender a relationship in which the balance of power is so unquestionably on their side.

If, after you earn the Ph.D., your chair seems unable or unwilling to tolerate an equitable relationship, you may find it preferable to allow the association to lapse rather than put up with being viewed as a "disciple" for the rest of your professional life. A sign of your growth as a thinker is that you have ceased simply echoing the authorities, and have learned to use their findings and insights as a departure point for developing your own authority. Some mentor-protégé relationships are catalysts for continued growth and others are tethers binding former students to junior status.

In part, because of the reluctance of mentors to let go, new Ph.D.s are advised against accepting positions in the departments from whence they came. Not that many have that opportunity, as it is widely believed that hiring one's own is intellectual incest.

Some Departments Make The Choice For You

The high potential value of the advisor-advisee relationship is widely recognized and there is a long and cherished tradition giving students the right and responsibility to select their own sponsors. Although this practice is customary, it is not a universal pattern by any means. Some departments simply assign dissertation chairs, leaving students no choice in the matter. Even when students have a choice, there is no guarantee that the person asked will agree to serve. Popular faculty members often have advising loads that preclude additional advisees, and sometimes the specialized nature of the topic severely limits the number of choices, especially in small departments.

DESIRABLE PROFESSIONAL CHARACTERISTICS

Whether you are free to seek whomever you want, or have to work with someone who is assigned, what are the most important professional characteristics of a chair?

Knowledge of the Field

Clearly, the person with whom you align yourself should be knowledgeable about the general field of inquiry which you plan to investigate. Look for a recognized authority in the same or closely-related area, one who has demonstrated expertise by publishing in a juried journal. It is a good bet that someone with recent publications will be acquainted with studies that are on the leading edge of the discipline and with seminal research in the field as well. Having already identified landmark investigations can save you hours of time. Even more important, it can help you formulate a research question that is currently in need of answers, one that can make an original contribution to theory, practice, or policy.

The "Full Bull"

Conventional wisdom has it that, in addition to a person with the appropriate expertise, the astute student will look for a tenured full professor, a "full bull." Full professors, the reasoning goes, are the powerbrokers of the department, in contrast to lower-ranking faculty who serve as workhorses. It is generally true that senior faculty sit in on the most influential committees, teach the preferred classes, and establish policy for the department and the university. They also make the tenure and promotion decisions about lower-ranking faculty. This greater independence and autonomy gives senior faculty members considerable clout over junior faculty members. All things being equal, this line of reasoning continues, they are in a better position to help their advisees navigate through any rough water they might encounter.

In addition to wielding influence within a particular setting, full professors usually have had more years in which to gain recognition in the wider world of scholarship, politics, business, and industry. Affiliation with a "giant" in a particular field offers enormous advantages in research possibilities and future job opportunities and it puts you in touch with people otherwise beyond your reach. You will be fortunate indeed if you can find a well-known figure to supervise your work and who will also be your advocate.

The BIG NAME

The advantages of working with giants notwithstanding, some big names can be inordinately preoccupied with their own research, publications, speaking engagements, consultancies, campus politics and the like. Full professors who have arrived, academically speaking, may be singularly disinterested in sponsoring a novice unless this person shows unusual promise as a research assistant or as a potential "disciple" who can make substantive contributions to the big name's own work. More than one doctoral candidate has discovered the typical *modus operandi*, that the student does all the work and the sponsor gets all of the credit. Nevertheless, if you think that you have something to offer a well-known scholar, who also seems to have an interest in you and your project, then by all means present this person with a dissertation idea which you think will capture her interest and which will make a strong case for you as a serious scholar.

Lesser Lights

As you check out the various faculty members, don't overlook the untenured professor who is urgently in need of publications in order to secure a tenure-track position. A tenure-seeking junior faculty member is nearly always on the lookout for doc students doing interesting research that might offer spin-offs for journal articles and conference presentations for the both of them. Co-authorship is a powerful incentive for faculty, especially if the student needs very little hand-holding.

Suppose you are planning to approach Dr. Z, an untenured prof in the department, whom you think is knowledgeable and with whom you communicate well. While it isn't wise to overlook him just because he has yet to achieve tenure, it is important not to *commit* yourself until you have determined his chances of sticking around a few years. As I mentioned in Chapter 3, Jill discovered that forming a relationship with someone on the way up is one thing, but forming a relationship with someone on the way out is quite another. Unless you are sure that she is going to be around when you need her, a safer choice is a tenured assistant professor or tenured associate bucking for full. Both are feeling the pressure to publish and will be attracted to a student who has something to contribute in exchange for the enormous amount of time it takes to properly supervise doctoral research.

DESIRABLE PERSONAL CHARACTERISTICS

Personal qualities are as important to consider as professional ones when you are looking over the faculty in search of a dissertation chair. Chairs can't be bypassed, ignored, or replaced by some another authority. They are integral to the process, so it behooves you to choose wisely. Ask yourself, is this person. . . .

Accessible? What good is a chair (even a very distinguished one) who makes you feel as if you were asking for an audience with the

Pope each time you suggest a meeting? You need someone who is personally, as well as professionally, accessible to you, who will return your phone calls before the next millennium, and who is inclined to see your success as a reflection of his or her own ability. Tap the student grapevine to discover which of the faculty are out of town a lot and ask the department chair or secretary who is planning a sabbatical leave in the near future.

Organized? The best chairs are also good managers who orchestrate the entire process by keeping you and your committee members on task and working in harmony. If you don't know from your own experience how well organized a potential chair is, make it your business to find out before making a commitment. Doctoral candidates unwise or unlucky enough to have chairs who habitually procrastinate, lose papers, give fuzzy feedback, or are chronically late returning manuscripts, face a problem of considerable magnitude.

Probably the most common complaint of doc students everywhere is the time it takes for their chairs to read and return manuscripts. When this turnaround time is excessively long and your unreturned manuscripts accumulate, months or even years can be lost. Even if you are one of the rare ones who aren't in a hurry to finish, you need timely feedback in order to keep you on track, and to maintain your forward momentum and enthusiasm.

What can you do with a chair who is slow to return your work? Actually, very little. Nagging is likely to be counter-productive. It is appropriate to inquire about the return of a manuscript two or three weeks after submission. If your polite inquiries continue to yield no response or a negative reaction, it is best to wait it out while trying to make progress on other fronts.

Don't make the mistake of pushing too hard for a short turnaround time. It makes no sense to sacrifice a thoughtful critique simply in the interest of time. Hurried, cursory readings of your manuscript will only cost you dearly in the long run. On the other hand, I have to admit that there is no guarantee a paper held for two months will be scrutinized any more carefully than one held for two weeks! Seek a chair who has the reputation for careful readings of manuscripts and reasonable turnaround times.

Warm and friendly? Here, a caveat is in order. A competent chair, even a mentor, doesn't have to be warm and friendly to be effective. Such appealing qualities can easily be overrated by an anxious candidate eager to find a compatible working relationship and in a hurry to finish.

Avoid the temptation to seek the most cordial person among the faculty who is easy to talk with yet whose standards may be less than rigorous. Certainly, you need to be able to communicate, but sometimes communication doesn't come readily or easily. The better student you are, the more you need a high-demand, no-nonsense type of research director who can stimulate you to perform at a level you never before thought possible. As I said before, faculty typically make the highest demands on their most capable students and consider this a compliment to the student's intellect! I admit that exacting taskmasters do not make a graduate student's hectic life any easier at the time, but it is the tough mentors who are remembered with gratitude, not the permissive ones.

EFFECTS OF "THE SYSTEM"

I have made much of the fact that even the most capable and amenable chair is constrained to some extent by "The System." A colleague in a prestigious university on the eastern seaboard regretfully summarizes this universal problem:

> Time spent with students doesn't show up on the books anywhere, so it doesn't count, not even as teaching. The implicit statement is that it isn't important and this is bound to be reflected in student-faculty relationships. Because the system really discourages it, it takes the most dedicated faculty member to commit high quality time to students. Many give them short shrift and concentrate instead on their own research which is rewarded by the administration.

PROFESSORS TO AVOID

The following isn't intended as a list of pure types that you will encounter on your way to the doctorate. As you trod those halls of ivy I hope you will never find a prof who matches these stereotypes exactly. I have typecast and deliberately exaggerated each portrayal in order to dramatize certain characteristics. Nevertheless, there is a grain of truth in each description.

Chair as Autocrat. This sponsor insists upon dictating your every move. If newly-emerged from student status, this person may use you to prove what a great scholar he is. Confusing authoritarianism with professionalism, such a chair can lead you on a not-so-merry chase before someone with more sense and experience steps in, if they ever do. The combination of authoritarianism and inexperience is especially deadly. Stay away from turkeys like this if you can, and if you find yourself in such a partnership, seriously consider the wisdom of changing chairs.

Not every autocrat is inexperienced, however. If your particular autocrat is also a knowledgeable and seasoned sponsor, the association may be worth the cost in your personal autonomy. Many busy dissertation chairs are reluctant to "waste" their own time by letting students explore ideas and methods with which they, the chair, disapprove or are unfamiliar. Having an autocratic chair isn't bad if you are in a hurry and willing to stifle some of your own ideas for the present. Chances are that you will reach your goal with very few glitches and will learn a lot about becoming a researcher in the process.

Chair as Judge and Jury. Initially, this category may seem very similar to the previous one, chair as autocrat, yet these two people are on opposite ends of the scale. Chair as judge offers you no help at all, just says aye or nay about everything you do, like a Roman emperor—thumbs up or thumbs down. The autocrat gives too much direction, the judge gives too little.

It takes an exceptionally able student who is also an experienced researcher to tolerate and survive such a relationship. Some other faculty member just might be willing to act as a kind of *de facto* chair in order to rescue you but don't count on it. More often, students caught in this unhappy situation have to scrounge for help and information across a wide array of sources or else look for another sponsor.

Chair as Opportunist. This person is looking for an academic slave to promote her own career. In exchange for sponsoring your dissertation you will be expected to be a research assistant and go-fer, on call whenever needed, regardless of your own deadlines. The worst of these opportunists will usurp your best ideas and fail to credit your contributions, knowing there isn't much you can do about it.

Chair as Sexist. Academe is no freer of sexist behaviors than the rest of the world and women encounter this unpleasant reality much more often than men. The more subtle it is, the harder it is to bear because the perpetrator can always feign innocence, claiming the victim is unduly sensitive to "womens' issues."

However, by the time they have reached graduate school, most women have learned to cope with sexism in its various forms, defending themselves when they have to and ignoring or avoiding it when possible. Fortunately, the most virulent of these types usually have already been identified by other grad students and you only have to tap the grapevine to learn who they are.

If, on the other hand, you are considering a professor who simply needs educating along these lines, perhaps you are just the one to roll up your sleeves and tackle the job.

Chair as Seducer or Seductress. Of all the types mentioned, this one is arguably the most dangerous to your professional goals and to your personal and emotional well-being. Student-chair relationships are difficult enough without the added complication of romantic intimacy. Nearly all universities recognize the vulnerability of both male and female students in this regard and have policies prohibiting sexual harassment and sexual liaisons between professors and students, at least while the student is under the professor's jurisdiction.

Less clear-cut is the issue of consensual relationships when the student is not directly under the professor's supervision. Even then, what might appear to be a consensual arrangement could actually be one of coercion because of the potential academic consequences of the relationship.

As a practical matter, it must be acknowledged that a few flirtations do culminate in permanent and presumably satisfying relationships. As a legal matter, the issue of consenting adults is cloudy at present. My advice is to stay out of such entanglements at least until you have secured your degree. Be a smart researcher, keep the probabilities on your side!

After offering you all of this good advice, I must confess that you may be in a small department, offering little choice among faculty members or perhaps in a large one where no one comes close to displaying the sterling attributes you are seeking. If this is the case, you will have to pick the lesser of two or more evils, find others to compensate for your chair's deficiencies and/or become extraordinarily self-sufficient. What happens if you decide the association is untenable?

"DIVORCING" YOUR CHAIR

Occasionally, a relationship between an advisor and advisee becomes so dysfunctional that the only way out is to dissolve it and seek a new sponsor. Usually difficult and sometimes painful, it is not impossible. Certainly, changing chairs should not be done capriciously, but only after you have made a sincere attempt to discuss, understand, and reconcile differences.

Consider the plight of Joy, a woman who was nearly immobilized by her feelings of anxiety and frustration:

> I am so intimidated by my chair's attitude that I usually leave our meetings without asking the questions I've gone in there to ask. I don't even know what his expectations are – only that I am not meeting them.
>
> If I weren't so afraid of antagonizing this guy, and the whole department to boot, I would look for a new sponsor!

Unquestionably, this is a relationship headed straight for disaster... for the student! Further discussion revealed that Joy was uncertain about how to change parts of her proposal the sponsor had simply labeled "inadequate." I understood her frustration but thought it was premature for her to be thinking about a new chair without a better

understanding of the problem with the current one, if indeed there was a problem. Knowing this man, I thought he might not be aware of her confusion, thinking he had made himself abundantly clear.

I insisted she initiate a frank discussion, despite her conviction that it wouldn't do any good. If this didn't work, I promised to advise her about terminating the relationship.

As it turned out, Joy was right. I learned through another source that her advisor was actively antagonistic to her for some reason and was convinced she wasn't "doctoral material." Instead of being forthright about his misgivings, he chose to discourage her progress by being uncommunicative.

Fortunately, another professor, Dr. S, had originally encouraged Joy to investigate this particular topic and was quite willing to take over as dissertation chair. Joy handled the situation by telling the first sponsor that she wanted to change the focus of her research and that Dr. S's interests were more compatible with this new direction. She was wise to put it in an academic, not a personal context.

It took a formal memo from the Dean's office and letters of confirmation to all parties, but the first sponsor was officially discontinued and the new sponsor appointed.

It is important to add that Joy's fear of heavy political fallout didn't materialize. The truth is that faculty are largely indifferent to such events unless they are directly involved. When a change of chairs is discreetly handled, the chances of alienating an entire department are essentially nil.

STRATEGIES FOR FINDING THE CHAIR YOU WANT

1. Take a Class From the Prof Under Consideration

For firsthand information, it is hard to beat taking a class from the professor under consideration, although liking someone's lectures is no guarantee you will like them as a director of research. Nevertheless, the class setting is a good place to learn about a potential chair's interactive style over a period of time and is a barometer of her depth of knowledge and ability to communicate in ways you find clear and stimulating. You can judge the timeliness with which papers are returned and the degree to which evaluations appear to be thoughtful, fair, and helpful.

Probably the biggest advantage of all is that it gives you direct personal access. Very few faculty will agree to sponsor you without knowing something about your academic interests and abilities.

Gilbert, who had gone back to school after ten years of managing his own business, put it this way:

> I took a course from Dr. O that was redundant for me just because I wanted access to her. It was worth the three units I had to spend because she is in such high demand that I knew I would have to make an exceptionally good impression if I were to have a chance of persuading her to be my chair.

2. Consult the Student Grapevine

The time-honored way to obtain information about faculty is to consult the student grapevine. An obvious disadvantage of this method is that other people's opinions are less dependable than your own first-hand experience, perceptions differing as they do. Someone viewed as too brusque by one student may be seen by another as simply businesslike and straightforward. With this forewarning in mind, however, the grapevine can be canvassed to yield valuable insights.

Students are actually more knowledgeable than faculty about some aspects of professorial behavior because they view it from an entirely different vantage point. A professor-to-student relationship is obviously quite different from a professor-to-professor relationship. Faculty who know a great deal about a colleague's professional reputation may be largely unaware of his attitudes and behaviors toward students.

In addition to being in a position to know, students are usually quite willing to share their experiences with their fellows, making the student network a very efficient vehicle for passing along information, relevant and not-so-relevant. More important, it is an excellent "socializing agent" for easing people into their roles as doctoral candidates. Find yourself a place in this network. Learn from it and contribute to it.

3. Ask Faculty About Faculty

Faculty, of course, have their own networks, but are considerably less than candid and more self-protective when discussing their colleagues, especially with students. They call this "being professional." Such reticence comes from the fact that, while students come and go, faculty expect to live with each other in the same institution (or discipline) over the years. Most profs don't have enough confidence in students' discretion to justify a fully candid evaluation of a colleague. A thoughtful listener, however, can often read between the lines. A professor who responds to your query about Dr. X by saying, "I think that Dr. Y's research is closer to your own interests," could be implying more than academic incompatibility.

UNDERSTANDING YOUR LEARNING STYLE

Before making that all-important choice of a chair, there is another matter that most individuals fail to consider. Accustomed over the years to being evaluated on *what* we learn, few of us consciously evaluate ourselves on *how* we learn. Knowledge of your learning style can develop into a kind of personal epistemology which is well worth the self-analysis it takes. Ask yourself, "do I perform better when I am given relatively free rein and allowed to work independently, or am I more confident with regular and frequent feedback?" Probably, most of us are in the latter category, no doubt conditioned by years of schooling in which regular evaluations have provided immediate feedback. I talked with two students who held opposing points of view in this matter. Student number one said,

> I don't want anyone to hover over me; that makes me crazy. At those times when I want help from my advisor, I will ask for it. I want an advisor who knows the field, who will inspire me to grow and change, but who will mostly leave me alone. I would rather set my own deadlines than have them imposed upon me.

Student number two responded in this way:

> I perform best with a certain amount of structure and have neither the time nor the energy to take a wrong turn and then have to recoup. As a single parent, I have obligations that many graduate students do not have so I want someone who will keep me on track each step of the way. I think I am doctoral caliber, whatever that means, but I may not fit the mold of the independent researcher that some professors have in mind.

The first student would do well with a chair who, after approval of the dissertation proposal, allows him to write large portions of the dissertation before submitting them for evaluation. Advisors who operate this way do so, not in deference to the independent learners among their students, but because it suits their own styles and schedules.

The second student would perform better with a chair who follows the more usual practice of evaluating drafts chapter by chapter. Neither way is intrinsically better than the other, despite the slightly apologetic tone of the student who needed more structure and feedback.

Happily, this is an instance in which there are many right ways to accomplish the same ends. You may think that independent learners are superior to structured learners (the latter sounding somewhat pedestrian) yet there are advantages and disadvantages to each learning style.

Independents sometimes venture too far ahead on their own, following a lead that ultimately reaches a dead end. Conversely, structured learners can become overly cautious and dependent upon expert opinion, inhibiting their own creativity and slowing their progress.

If you are a compulsively conscientious student, you may be primarily in need of unflagging emotional support and an occasional suggestion. If you have an abundance of ideas but little sense of direction, you may benefit from finding someone who can provide both discipline and focus.

Perfect matches may be made in heaven but don't look for them on college campuses! Most of you will have to settle for a chair who meets only a few of your highest priorities.

HOW TO CONVINCE A PROFESSOR TO SPONSOR YOU

Now let us suppose you have identified someone with whom you wish to work. The next step is to convince this person that you can generate ideas worthy of a dissertation research project and that you have both the skills and the dedication to do the job. Busy faculty are reluctant to take on doctoral candidates who require spoon-feeding or who, at the other extreme, are so independent that they bristle with resentment at each constructive criticism. Without question, they would prefer to invest their time and energy with self-reliant, diligent people who show professional promise. Surrounding themselves with high caliber students is one way to enhance their own scholarly reputations.

A few days before you meet with the prof, send him a written sample of your research ideas, perhaps even including some possible methodologies. Your thoughtfulness will be appreciated and you will be presenting yourself as a serious student even if he doesn't find time to do more than glance at your note before you meet. More important, make it a point to read his most recent publications beforehand and mention any finding, methodology, or theory that has implications for your own investigation. Such a demonstration of familiarity with his work is more than subtle flattery it is *prima-facie* evidence that you do your homework. Especially if you have had little contact with this person, these suggestions, together with your powers of oral persuasion, will help him view you in a favorable light. Several considerations will influence the decision: the way you present yourself and your ideas, your reputation in the department, the prof's interest in the topic, and whether he has the time to supervise your dissertation research.

SELECTING THE REST OF THE COMMITTEE

In departments where you are expected to find your own chair you are usually expected to choose committee members as well. Occasionally however, your chair will want to "sound out" potential committee members before you approach them. In a few settings it is customary for the department chair to assign professors to students' dissertation committees, but this is relatively rare.

The Importance of the Chair's Input

In your search for people to make up the rest of the committee, rely heavily on your chair's knowledge of colleagues. Despite the fact that they play a subsidiary role as second, third, or fourth reader, committee members should have essentially the same qualities you sought in a chair, albeit with different areas of expertise. As you discuss the various possibilities with your chair, the implicit, unasked question becomes, "Can you, my dear chair, work productively with this person?"

Consider an Outsider

Relying on your chair's judgment doesn't mean you should abdicate your right to shape this group when you can. Explore possibilities outside the department that the chair might not be aware of. Perhaps you have maintained contact with someone from your undergraduate days or you may have heard of a prominent authority on your particular topic who is entirely outside the university community. People in business, government, medical labs, and think tanks are often pleased to forge linkages with universities and they can infuse your project with a fresh point of view. Outsiders are more likely to enhance than disrupt the orderly workings of the committee, in part because they have no negative history with other members.

TECHNICAL HELP

What kinds of expertise do you need? Unless you are supremely confident of your statistical knowledge, you will be wise to include a statistician-methodologist in the group, even if your chair does not suggest it. Previous courses, even if you did well, are seldom adequate to the task. A specialist is needed because the collective experience of committees is often limited to commonly used procedures in investigations they have either conducted themselves or supervised. Someone familiar with a broad range of statistical treatments can help you select the techniques most suitable for your particular problem.

In addition, a statistician on your team is particularly useful during the defense of the thesis should someone challenge a fine point in the analysis. In most cases, however, committee members won't even question your methodology if they know the work has passed the scrutiny of a respected statistician-methodologist. While you must be able to defend your own procedures, having a statistician to back you up is simply good insurance.

If no such person is available, or if the committee is already filled with essential constituents, the next best thing is to hire a consultant. Be warned that a few departments or dissertation chairs still hold that hiring technical help is, somehow, cheating. It seems to me that students can reasonably expect the program to prepare them for doing doctoral-level research. If it doesn't, there should be no prohibition against finding ways to compensate for this deficiency. Faculty use consultants all the time; if they didn't there would be far fewer research projects conducted on university campuses.

Clearly, my indignation or yours will do little to change the situation if your department frowns upon hired consultants. Some students I interviewed found non-monetary ways to compensate consultants, assuming informal, unpaid help could be better justified. An expert typist typed her friend's dissertation in exchange for his help with multivariate statistical techniques. Another coached a friend for his language exam in exchange for her advice on methods of restoring Byzantine mosaics.

The trick is, of course, to find someone who is willing to swap skills with you. If you can afford to pay for technical help, and it doesn't violate policy, this arrangement is cleaner, quicker, and far more satisfactory, in my opinion.

Understand the Stats

No matter where your technical help comes from, however, it is absolutely imperative that you *thoroughly understand* how your data are being analyzed, why certain treatments are used, and what their limitations are.

Suppose, for example, you decide to determine the relationship between test anxiety and test performance by calculating a correlation coefficient. You are assuming a linear (straight-line) relationship in which the greater the anxiety, the poorer the test performance and vice versa. Our hypothetical consultant is now about to earn his or her keep by reminding you that the relationship between these two variables may not be linear at all, but rather *curvilinear*, as shown below.

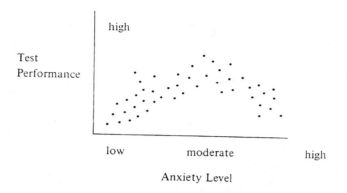

A curvilinear relationship, in this case, occurs when people with moderate anxiety levels tend to outperform those with either high or low anxiety levels. Here, a correlation coefficient would be inappropriate, indicating a low, non-significant relationship when actually a strong but curvilinear relationship existed.

Horror Stories of Internecine Warfare

Your first consideration in building a committee is to include an adequate assortment of intellectual resources; your second is to find people who can work together in relative harmony. Sooner or later, everybody does have to agree on everything that goes into your dissertation and you must have heard horror stories about candidates caught in the crossfire between two feuding committee members.

It is true that one chronic nay-sayer can be a major aggravation and one procrastinator can cost you months of valuable time. Conversely, a strong personal advocate can build consensus and even compensate for a weak or unreasonable committee member. Your best protection against warring factions is a strong, well-respected, supportive chair who won't let faculty squabbles get out of hand.

Keeping in Touch With Faculty and Staff

How often should you touch base with members of your committee? There are two schools of thought about this. One advises you to maintain close contact with your chair and each committee member so as to keep everybody posted on your progress and provide opportunities for feedback.

The other school of thought advises you to maintain close contact *only with your chair* (and methodologist, if you have one), limiting your contact with the rest of the committee as much as possible and letting your chair negotiate on your behalf.[2]

The advice you take depends upon the chair you have. Many chairs are too busy to act as mediators except on major issues and are particularly reluctant to intrude on a colleague's academic turf. Further, they like to share the responsibility while reserving the right to pass final judgment.

On the other hand, a powerful chair with a committee willing to turn over most of the responsibility can certainly expedite things for you. The primary risk is that some member of the committee will object to a major premise late enough in the process to force you to undertake a major overhaul.

Whatever you do, keep a high profile in the department. Get acquainted with office personnel and other students. Schedule regular meetings with your chair and, as wisdom dictates, with committee members. Don't be a pest but do be a "presence" and use chance encounters to keep up your visibility. Brief informal exchanges in the halls, on the campus, and even in the rest rooms offer opportunities to keep a high profile in the department. To the extent you are effective in building a strong base of support, you will guard against unwelcome surprises.

WORKING WITH YOUR CHAIR

As I said at the beginning of this chapter, your relationship with your chair is the most important relationship you will make during your student career. Because of its significance, it is often compared to a love affair, albeit a platonic one. While this may be putting it too strongly, it is safe to say, the better the relationship in terms of intellectual substance, the more apt it is to have a strong emotional component as well. Each person has an investment in the other, although from a student perspective it may seem largely one-sided. I have found that student-chair relationships are least apt to be meaningful in those impersonal academic settings known as "diploma mills," where the student is already being shortchanged in other ways.

Working Arrangements

Let us start with practical matters. At the outset, it is important to get a clear understanding about how your chair wants to operate. Are you to submit drafts chapter by chapter or wait until you have a draft of the entire dissertation? Must you proceed in standard *seriatim* order or can you write and submit the "meaty" chapters, e.g., data collection, methods and procedures, first? Does your chair want to see everything you write before you present it to others on the committee or can you distribute at least some chapters simultaneously? How much, or little, contact are you expected to maintain with the rest of the committee?

As a graduate student striving to satisfy an individual professor, you have learned to accept criticism as part of the SOP. Now, as a doctoral candidate, you have to satisfy not one but eventually three or four professors. With revisions a foregone conclusion, try to negotiate a plan whereby you submit each chapter to your thesis director as it is completed. Although the others will have to approve it eventually, simultaneous submission to all parties is inefficient and confusing because of the high probability of receiving contradictory suggestions for revisions. Chapters which have been revised under the direction of your chair will suffer less annihilation at the hands of committee members. Distribute these chapters as soon as possible after your chair has approved them and be sure to tell each committee member that the chair has approved. It is to your advantage to get the committee's O.K. soon, just in case one of them gets contentious about the representativeness of your sample or takes issue with your basic theoretical premise.

Keep Your Eye on the Maestro

Chairs, as maestros of their respective orchestras, are responsible for any sour notes that are struck. This makes them extremely protective of their authority. No matter how good your rapport might be with another committee member, never bypass your chair for any reason. Don't even work independently with the statistician or methodologist without your chair's knowledge and approval.

Bob, a doctoral student in physical anthropology, learned this lesson the hard way. He was comparing skull measurements between two ancient American Indian tribes and had the beginnings of a good relationship with his chair before committing the following faux pas:

> Here I am in the student union, drinking coffee and going over a computer printout with Dr. L who is on my committee and whose field is statistics. Just then my thesis director walked in. Oh, he saw us all right, but just glowered and walked right by our table without even speaking. Well, Dr. L gave me this funny look, handed back the printout, said she had another appointment, and walked away.
>
> My advisor seemed different after that, cooler and more critical. Finally, I couldn't stand it any longer and explained that Dr. L had been helping me in the interpretation of paired comparisons. Well, my chair gave me to understand in no uncertain terms that *he* was running this show, not the third reader! I can't understand this attitude. What's the big deal?

The big deal is that the buck stops at the chair's desk. Each dissertation supervised is a direct reflection upon the chair's scholarship, and, to a lesser degree, on the reputation of the committee, the department, and the university. Some chairs, if consulted, are happy to turn over certain specialized aspects of the research to the "technicians," but none will give up control. So, remember to keep your eye on the maestro.

Initiating Contact With Your Chair

Unless your chair says directly, "Don't call me, I'll call you," it will be up to you to initiate all contacts. Don't be a nuisance or too aggressive, but do be assertive. Too many students fear they are intruding upon a prof's time and fail to claim the time that is rightfully due them. Intending to demonstrate consideration, they are likely to be seen as disinterested. Better be labeled too pushy than too laid-back.

Try to schedule regular meetings, once a week if you are a full-time student, and less often if you are part-time. Be obliging and flexible in adjusting to your chair's calendar and plan carefully in order to get maximum mileage out of the time you spend together.

First Impressions

Remember the importance of first impressions. Establish yourself as a serious student right off the bat by submitting thoughtful, coherent, clean, and finished-looking first drafts even though you know you will probably be writing this paper again and again. Academics spend many tedious hours reading student papers and resent having to struggle through misspellings, typos, sloppy thinking, and excessive jargon. It is very hard to redeem yourself after a carelessly written first presentation, even if the rewrite is well done.

On the other hand, don't be so much of a perfectionist that you compulsively polish your manuscript endlessly and never think it is good enough. You can't be expected to write a publishable paper on the first try, but you can, from the very first paper, be sure that your work is grammatical, well-punctuated, and free of misspellings and typos. Because most dissertations are technical reports of empirical investigations, you must say what you mean simply and concisely, avoiding pedantry and "dissertationese!"

Keeping hard copies of your work is as necessary as it is easy. At this point in your academic career, you have probably had the unhappy experience of losing computer data. Before you log off, form a habit of making a back-up copy of everything you did at that particular sitting.

Give Readers Time to Read Your Manuscripts

There is nothing quite as irritating to a prof as a student who turns in a manuscript on Friday saying he needs it back by Monday. Never mind that this same prof may urge you to turn in a paper promptly only to let it sit on his desk for weeks. Differing perceptions of timeliness are the source of much conflict between students and faculty. After two or three diplomatically phrased inquiries, your only recourse is to wait as patiently as possible, hoping that the wait will be justified by a thorough and helpful reading. As you grin and bear it, resolve not to thoughtlessly repeat this behavior when your turn comes around.

The Gentle Art of Compensation

University campuses are fertile with a wide variety of talented individuals who can be called upon for information, dialogue, inspiration, and fellowship. In the aggregate, they can compensate for qualities missing in your chair. A committee member may be willing to brainstorm a particularly vexing problem, someone outside of your committee may provide technical information, the department secretary may be able to get a signature from a hard-to-reach administrator, and a fellow student can be there for that much-needed gripe session. Spouses, lovers, friends, and families are in a special category and will be discussed in the last chapter.

No matter how well you cultivate and expand your garden of human resources, it is your chair who has the final say. As a rule, chairs try to facilitate their candidate's progress, although there are wide variations in the degree of effort and commitment they devote to this responsibility. Generally speaking, the higher the quality of your work, the better you make your sponsor look and the more support you can expect.

As in any meaningful human relationship, both partners contribute to its success or failure. Probably, the real caliber of the affiliation will not become apparent for several years after the degree has been awarded. It is a bit like parenting; you don't really appreciate the fine points until you go through the same experience.

Despite the absence of extrinsic rewards, a surprising number of faculty seem to derive intrinsic satisfaction out of helping students become scholars. If you are fortunate enough to find such a person, and if you do your part to nourish the relationship, 20 years from now, memories of your experience may evoke feelings similar to those of a colleague of mine who said:

> The union between student and mentor is like a love affair, but without the physical intimacy. Whether it is two men, two women, or a man and woman, the relationship often is intimate and emotionally charged. It can be troubled with jealousy or made pleasant with affection . . . it can work either way. The affection is subliminal and non-pathological for the most part. This is natural because you are on a long trip in a small boat together. You cannot be that close, working long hours literally elbow to elbow, and not develop a kinship.

SUMMARY

Your academic future rides on the judgment of the members of your committee, particularly your dissertation chair, which makes selection of this person highly important. While few students find a real *mentor*, one who cares deeply about their well-being, most find someone who will serve as an adequate guide through the process.

Look for a person who is knowledgeable in your field, personally accessible, well organized, and with whom you feel some degree of rapport. However, don't confuse rapport with integrity or ability. The better student you are, the more you will need a no-nonsense, demanding taskmaster who will challenge you to do your best.

The most obvious choice is not always the best choice. Big names may be too busy with their own careers to devote enough time to advisees, although a giant in your field, who is really interested in you, can be a great asset now and after graduation. While academe has its share of autocrats, exploiters, and sexists, the most common problem is faculty indifference. The university system rewards professors for producing their own research, not for supervising yours.

Yes, "divorcing" your chair is possible after a sincere attempt has been made to work things out, but needs to be carefully and discreetly handled.

To find a chair, take a class, consult the student grapevine, or even ask a faculty member, although this is less likely to yield a candid response. Once you have decided upon whom to approach, present yourself as a self-reliant, serious student, a person likely to enhance the prof's own career. Your chair's input will help you select the rest of the committee. Important unspoken questions are: "Can you, dear chair, work well with these people, and do you think they can work with each other?" Your dissertation sponsor is the maestro who directs this particular orchestra, so nourish this relationship with intelligence and care.

NOTES

1. Blackwell, J. E.: Mentoring: An Action Strategy for Increasing Minority Faculty. Academe, 75: 8, 1989. In this article professors from various U.S. academic institutions engage in a dialogue with Blackwell about academic policies and practices.
2. Rudestam, K. E. and Newton, R. R.: Surviving Your Dissertation: A Comprehensive Guide to Content and Process. Newbury Park, Sage, 1992, p. 132.

Chapter 5

WRITING THE PROPOSAL

I was talking with a group of students at a large urban university about the ups and downs of doctoral study. After a couple of hours, what had been a lively exchange began to wane and I noticed several people looking at their watches. Someone suggested we adjourn to the cafeteria and continue our discussion over lunch. I agreed, knowing the group would thin out and people would be willing to say things in the small group that they wouldn't say in the large one. My hunch was right. Soon after we were seated, Chris, a candidate for a Ph.D. in education, declared with some heat:

> I didn't want to mention it earlier, but there are two people in our study group who are already running experiments while the rest of us are still trying to get our proposals approved. My advisor and I have agreed on my project so I don't need a formal process. Why should some get a head start just because they're in a department where a formal proposal isn't required?

Like Chris, you may be eager to plunge into your research project and start gathering data and testing hypotheses. Having passed prelims (or quals), you have little patience with what looks like an extra step in an already lengthy process, but let us look at the advantages.

THE MANY FUNCTIONS OF A PROPOSAL

The primary purpose of a formal dissertation proposal is to spell out exactly what you plan to do and how you plan to do it. It states the *sig-*

nificance of the problem, identifies the *dimensions* of the problem, and describes the *methods* that will be used to solve the problem.

As a Way to Save Time

An approved proposal allows you to proceed with greater speed and confidence because you don't have to clear each step along the way with your sponsor. Then once you have conducted the study, with very little additional effort you can convert your proposal into the first three chapters of your finished dissertation. This saves you time in the long run.

As a Contract Between You and the Faculty

Written agreements, in contrast to oral ones, help avoid misunderstandings and provide protection for all parties to the transaction. In this case the protection is especially for you, the candidate. You may fear that writing a proposal when it is not required implies mistrust of your chair and risks demeaning that important relationship. I can only say that such a reaction on the part of a sponsor is highly unlikely. On the contrary, the misunderstandings that arise out of failure to be specific are more apt to pose a danger to the advisor/advisee relationship. I can almost guarantee that your chair will be favorably impressed by your willingness to formulate a reasoned, methodical, and detailed plan of action.

Do not fear that you will be irrevocably locked into every detail of your original proposal, bound by a contract that can be changed only by your committee. As a matter of fact, most of the ideas for improvement will probably be your own. Modifications are most likely to be needed in data-gathering procedures, data management, and in methods used to test relationships between and among variables.

Serendipity is always an exciting possibility. I am not talking about chance in the statistical sense of unexplained variance, of course, but of finding something valuable and unexpected among commonplace and expected outcomes. This sense of pending discovery is one of the most rewarding aspects of empirical research, compensating for the painstaking attention that must be paid to every detail. Interestingly, serendipitous findings occasionally turn out to be more important than those originally sought.

As an Insurance Policy

Perhaps the most important result of going to all the trouble of securing an approved proposal is that it provides one of the few substantive guarantees available to you in the uncertain world of doctoral study. It signifies the faculty's willingness to award the degree if the contract is fulfilled within the allotted time. This is important because no matter how well you have chosen your committee, or how good the rapport among you, there is absolutely no assurance that any of these people will remain in position until you finish as the following story will illustrate.

The group of students who had been almost unanimous in their objections to the proposal requirement up to this point, fell silent when one man began to relate a story about a friend's experience.

> My friend, Sam, and his sponsor were working on a city schools project evaluating different math learning strategies that Sam was going to use as a basis for his dissertation. Things were going well until Dr. H's wife came down with leukemia and he took a leave to spend all his time with her. He lost interest in everything: his job, his life outside the hospital, and, of course, Sam's dissertation. Not that anyone could blame him.

It was a small department where only one other person had connections with the city schools and that person was unwilling (or maybe unable) to take over. Everything was in writing and no proposal was finalized. Sadly, Sam never got his degree and now is back to teaching Jr. High.

An approved proposal also offers protection against a disinterested or downright hostile committee member. Some advisors speculate (albeit without supporting data) that an approved proposal is the distinguishing feature separating those candidates who finish from those who don't.

As Preparation for Grant-Writing

Among the advantages of a formal proposal is one seldom mentioned, the experience it offers in grant-writing. As you know, grant-seeking is a way of life in academe. Professors must "buy" themselves released time from teaching in order to research and write. Indeed, new Ph.D.s who have a research grant in hand in addition to a degree will find their chances of locating a position greatly improved. Now is the perfect time to cultivate your skills while you have faculty critics to help and under conditions less competitive than when you are a junior faculty member vying with experienced academics for scarce grant monies.

As the First Three Chapters of Your Dissertation

Another benefit of an approved proposal is that the first three chapters can be converted, with a few changes, to form the first three chapters of your dissertation. The first chapter (Introduction to the Problem via the Abstract) and the second chapter (Review of the Literature), can be used almost verbatim with a tense change here and a bit of editing there. Chapter 3 (Method) will need more attention and must await the gathering and analysis of data.

Now let us turn to a simple, but important question: what are dissertations supposed to do?

DISSERTATION EXPECTATIONS

Dissertation styles and formats differ considerably across disciplines and departments and among dissertation advisors. Whether you conduct a basic, experimental, applied, evaluative, ethnographical, archival, or historical study depends upon what your discipline, department, and chair deem appropriate. Although you will be subject to the predilections of your advisor and even the fashion of the moment, all dissertations share common goals.

The time-honored dictum describing the purpose of a dissertation is to address at least one of the following:

> . . . uncover new facts or principles, suggest relationships that were previously unrecognized, challenge existing truths or assumptions, afford new insights into little-understood phenomena, or suggest new interpretations of known facts that alter man's perceptions of the world around him.[1] (Madsen, David: *Successful Dissertations and Theses: A Guide*

to Graduate Student Research from Proposal to Completion. San Francisco, Jossey-Bass, 1983)

While I have no quarrel with this advice as an ideal, as something to strive for, I think it asks a lot of a doctoral candidate. Few experienced researchers are able to make this kind of an impact on their disciplines.

If you followed my recommendations in Chapter 4, you already have an outline which you used to convince a professor your project was worth supporting. Now, still using an outline format, fill in the major elements in your design in greater detail to present to your chair. Unless the chair objects, I suggest you continue to use an outline form, instead of a narrative, until the major components of your plan are in place (an outline highlights the main concepts and is more easily modified than a narrative).

Expect to rewrite your draft several times until it describes exactly what you want to do and meets with your chair's approval. After the two of you have agreed, and before showing the outline to the rest of the committee, convert it into narrative form in a fully detailed formal proposal with such appropriate headings as: The Problem, Review of the Literature, and Method.

The usual procedure is to submit the draft to each committee member individually. There may be more revisions, but these are typically minimal compared to those required after the chair's scrutiny. Moreover, it is not always necessary to follow each committee member's suggestions verbatim. Indeed, professors using the time-honored practice of brainstorming do not always expect each idea to be pursued to its logical conclusion. Some comments are intended to be more provocative than compelling, although you need to be clear about which comments are suggestions and which are requirements. Sift ideas through your own cognitive filter, and be sure to confer with your sponsor before making significant changes in the design or methodology on the recommendation of a single committee person.

THE ELEMENTS OF A PROPOSAL

Forms may vary, but all proposals contain certain common elements. These include:

1. Cover Page
2. Abstract
3. The Problem (Chapter 1)
4. Review of the Literature (Chapter 2)
5. Method (Chapter 3)
6. Results and Recommendations for Further Research

Cover Page

The cover page contains the proposed title of the study together with your name, address, and phone number; department and university; names of your advisor and committee; and the date the proposal is submitted.

Title

A good title is brief, descriptive, and appealing to potential readers. Draft the most descriptive title you can think of at the start and let it evolve right along with the investigation.

A common problem with dissertation titles is that they attempt too much. Consider this gem: "A Study of the Efficacy of Vocational Interest Inventories Versus Personality Inventories Using Multivariate Analysis in the Prediction of Job Satisfaction for Adults, Aged 18 to 24 in Their First Year of Employment."

Leave information about the nature of subjects, instrumentation, and statistical procedures for the Method chapter and avoid using such superfluous lead phrases as, "A Study of," "An Analysis of," or "A Comparison of." Try to phrase the title so that a prospective reader can tell in a glance what the dissertation is about.

Abstract

Writing this summary is an extremely important part of the entire undertaking. Your abstract will appear in the Dissertation Abstracts International to be read by other scholars searching the research literature for questions and answers pertaining to their own research efforts. A single page or less must tell the whole story.

Because it is so difficult to encompass all of the important elements in a short coherent statement, it is best to wait until the results are in and reported in full before trying to put your entire project in this scholarly nutshell.

The Research Problem

Identification and discussion of the problem to be solved serves as an introduction to your investigation. Some scholars distinguish between the statement of the problem (e.g., a study of the relationship between birth order and achievement needs), and the research question (do first-born children have stronger achievement needs than their younger siblings?). Your dissertation chair is sure to have an opinion on this issue.

Emerging logically from the statement and/or question are the hypotheses, typically written in the null or no-significant-difference form.

This section will be longer than the single-page abstract, anywhere from two to eight pages. Some advisors want you to begin this section by providing a general background to orient the reader to the significance of the problem as well as to place it in context with previous work in the discipline.

More and more, however, advisors want students to follow the journal article practice of plunging immediately into the heart of the matter, briefly explaining the significance of the problem and citing a few pertinent references. Contextual matter can follow to orient the reader more thoroughly. Journal style favors brevity over loquaciousness, although it must be *comprehensive* brevity. Writing briefly, but comprehensively, requires you to be thoroughly familiar with seminal (probably early) and cutting-edge (probably recent) research pertinent to your problem. A well-developed statement of the problem or research question is a result of sifting through a mountain of other people's findings to extract those few questions which you want to address.

The following examples illustrate ways to present the problem. In example No. 1, the problem is posed as a general question followed by more specific queries:

   Example No. 1. What is the relationship between health-oriented behaviors and the education level of adult Americans?
   a. Are college-educated people better informed about good health practices than high school-educated people?

b. What is the relationship between knowing the facts about healthful practices and engaging in such practices on a daily basis?

Another way to present the problem is to directly pose the hypotheses, as in Example No. 2:

Example No. 2. This investigation is designed to test the following propositions:
a. There is a correlation of less than .40 between the pass rate of individuals taking the behind-the-wheel driving test and their written driving test.
b. There is a correlation of less than .10 between the age and pass rate of drivers renewing their driver's licenses.

Example No. 3 poses the problem in yet another way, as a statement followed by questions:

Example No. 3. There is a significant relationship between bilingualism and self concept.
a. Do college students who are fluent in a language other than English, achieve higher scores on the Tennessee Self Concept Scales than those who speak only English?
b. Is there a significant difference in scores on the Tennessee Self Concept Scales among people whose second language is Spanish, French, or German?

Review of the Literature

Elinor had spent weeks researching professional journals, books, and dissertations in her field of public health. In the process she had accumulated an impressive list of references, carefully annotated.

I was shocked when my advisor told me not to include my whole bibliography in my dissertation. When my brother went through this department his chair considered the lit review to be a major part of the dissertation.

My chair says it is important too, so how come he wants only eight references in the body of my dissertation, about a dozen in the Appendix, and the rest he says to save for another study?

While advisors differ on how many references to include, they all agree that a proper literature review calls for more than a list of your readings while you were searching for a dissertation topic.

There is a growing trend for sparse, sharply focused lit reviews such as Elinor's sponsor wanted. Your chair may suggest that you omit a large percentage of the articles you have read with such diligence and care.

Many students are reluctant to do this, wanting instead to preserve evidence of long hours spent in research. Believe me, the evidence will be there indirectly, in your command of the subject in the context of previous inquiries. Resist the temptation to include page after page of references. A list of tangentially-related citations is a distraction, while a composite of pertinent articles will funnel the reader's thinking directly to the problem itself.

Some advisors suggest postponing the lit review until after your investigation is complete. This is because there seems to be a natural progression from *abstract* questions to *concrete* ways of asking them. This natural progression is interrupted when you stop to read research reports, even when they are pertinent. Advisors who hold this point of view maintain that you will learn more about the phenomenon you are studying by conducting an empirical investigation of your own than you ever could by reading other's research.[2]

I agree that hands-on experience is the best teacher, although learning in this way will probably be less broadly based than more ecumenical readings. When my own advisees are reasonably knowledgeable about the literature in the field they intend to investigate, I suggest they plunge right into the task of proposal writing. Once underway, the project seems to generate its own momentum in harmony with some kind of internal logic.

Method

This is the place for a detailed description of your population and sample, measurement instruments, kinds of data to be gathered, methods for gathering data, and statistical techniques to be used for analysis. It is also the section where you establish your study in context with a good theoretical or conceptual framework to answer the inevitable "so what?" question. You have formulated the problem, you have collected and analyzed the data, you have drawn conclusions and made recommendations—so what? What difference does it make? What are the theoretical and practical implications? Think about the "so what?" question all the way through your project, because it will surely come up during your oral defense in some form.

BASIC RESEARCH CONCEPTS

The following brief discussion of basic research concepts and procedures is intended to reinforce what you already know and to present a structure for the methods chapter. It is not a substitute for a statistics text, and you must look elsewhere for information about specialized techniques designed for specific fields and problems.

Population

A population is the total group of individuals (units, cases, groups, or events) that display the characteristics you intend to study and about which you wish to make inferences. The more specific the characteristics, the more restricted the population. If you are investigating professional U.S. tennis players, the population is all of the people in the U.S. who play tennis professionally. If you narrow the criteria to professional tennis players under the age of 30, the population becomes more restricted. Adding another variable (perhaps gender) would further restrict the group about which you seek to make inferences.

Sample

A subset of cases drawn from the population is called a sample. You are interested in examining certain characteristics in an entire population, but you haven't resources or time enough to test each individual. Sampling enables you to make these inferences, that is to *generalize* about selected attributes of the large group on the basis of information obtained from the small group. This can be accomplished with the aid of statistics if the sample is based on a *probabilistic* strategy as in random sampling.

Random Sampling

Random sampling is the most basic type of probability sampling. It is a subset drawn from the population in such a manner that each individual unit has an equal chance of being selected. For example, pollsters seeking to predict the outcome of a district election ask a random sample of voters within the district how they intend to vote. Using this information, pollsters can generalize from the small group to the larger one and predict the outcome of the election within a specific margin of error. Assuming the respondents are truthful (and their behavior matches their words), the more representative the sample, the more accurate the prediction.

Random sampling can be accomplished through the use of a table of random numbers. First, assign a number to each case in your population. Then, with a table of random numbers in hand (most statistics texts have them in appendices), select numbers consecutively as they appear in the table by starting at any column or row, left to right, right to left, upward, downward, or diagonally across. Continue to select numbers in order until you have obtained enough for your sample and then pick the corresponding numbers in the population. Computer programs can be used for this simple-minded but arduous task.

Stratified Random Sampling

The preferred method of most behavioral scientists is the use of stratified random sampling. This requires the breakdown of the population into separate groups or "strata" on the basis of certain criteria, say economics. One strata could be below $10,000; another between $10,000 and $40,000; another between $40,000 and $60,000, etc. The stratification need not be hierarchical. It could be groups of people from different ethnic backgrounds, or political parties or religious groups.

Within each stratum, a random sample is drawn. The procedure is most effective when each stratum is homogeneous in regard to the variables of interest so that sample size can be relatively small. Sometimes that is a decided advantage. As a sampling method, stratified random sampling has an advantage over simple random sampling because it incorporates important variables by using them to define the strata.

Disproportionate Sampling

Another refinement of random sampling makes it possible to generalize from samples drawn from populations differing widely in the number of people in each group or stratum. Suppose you are studying the effects of students' ethnic background on their endorsement of gun control at a college where Anglos and Asian Americans predominate but where there are relatively few African Americans, Hispanics, and Native Americans. Taking 10 percent from each stratum would yield so few African Americans, Hispanics, and Native Americans as to make their responses statistically unstable. These groups are relevant to your study, so you don't want to ignore them and the other option, doubling or tripling the number of respondents in all five groups would be too costly.

The technique of disproportionate sampling allows you to work with disproportionate numbers by assigning *weights* to each ethnic group corresponding to that group's relative proportion in the population from which they were drawn.

Let us assume you have decided that a sample of 100 people in each stratum will be sufficient to test your hypothesis. Row *B* in Table I shows these 100 students and row *D* shows the *number* who say they are in favor of gun control. In this case, the raw number also represents the *percentage* of people giving a positive response. You can see, for example, that 90 percent of Asian Americans and 60 percent of Native Americans say they are in favor of gun control legislation.

Table I

THE EFFECTS OF ETHNICITY ON ATTITUDES TOWARD
GUN CONTROL STRATIFIED WEIGHTED RANDOM SAMPLE

	Anglo	*Asian A.*	*African A.*	*Hispanic*	*Native A.*	*Total*
A. Population	3300	1500	1000	1000	300	7100
B. Sample	100	100	100	100	100	500
C. Percent of Population	46.5	21.1	14.1	14.1	4.2	100
D. No. favoring gun control	80	90	70	80	60	380
E. Inferred no. favoring gun control						
(D x A)	2640	1350	700	800	180	5670
F. Inferred % in favor of gun control						
(D x C)	37.2	19	9.9	11.3	2.5	80

Now, if you simply took all 380 students who said they favored gun control (the total of row *D*) and divided by the total number of students (500) you would infer that 76 percent of the students in that college favored gun control and you would be wrong. This is because you failed to take into account the large differences in the number of people in the original strata from which the sample was drawn (row *A*).

In order to adjust for disproportionate sizes in populations you must multiply the percentage of students favoring gun control in each stratum (row *D*) by the percentage (weight) that stratum is of the total (row *C*). Now you see that an inference of 80 percent, (or 5,670 students) favoring gun control legislation is a better estimate.

Sampling Error

Since it is nearly impossible to select a sample that represents with perfect fidelity all of the attributes, behaviors, and relationships of interest in the entire population, generalization (prediction) always involves errors. Expecting errors, you try to keep them within a known and acceptable range by choosing a sample large enough to minimize sampling error. Generally speaking, the larger the sample the better the estimate of the population. You also must select a statistical treatment powerful enough to detect any significant differences that may be present. Sample size and statistical power bear directly upon the outcome of your inquiry and there are books and monographs devoted to making these choices. One of the best is entitled "How Many Subjects: Statistical Power Analysis in Research."[3]

Sampling Bias

Probably the most classic example of bias is an event that shocked the nation way back in 1936 when the *Literary Digest* confidently predicted (based on a massive 2,000,000 poll of individuals) that Alfred Landon would beat Franklin Roosevelt in his race for a second term as president. The sample was drawn from telephone directories and automobile registration lists. This had worked out well in predicting election results in 1920, 1924, 1928, and 1932, so the "experts" thought they would surely work again. No one realized that the sample group didn't accurately reflect the voting public. Lower-income people, who couldn't afford phones and cars, turned out en masse to vote the Democratic ticket.

Many hadn't voted in the years between 1920 and 1932, but the Great Depression had realigned them along socioeconomic lines and they voted in 1936.

Pollsters learned two things from this disaster: one, a large sample doesn't necessarily prevent bias, and two, a non-representative sample can cause great embarrassment!

HUMAN SUBJECTS

Unless you are conducting an archival study or using non-reactive research methodology such as measuring the erosion of floor tiles to indicate interest in museum exhibits, you will need to locate and employ human subjects. Carefully selected, your sample can generalize to the population you plan to investigate. Before committing yourself to any source, ask yourself how they may differ from the population to which you want to generalize. Are you mixing volunteers responding to a newspaper ad with friends who might be sympathetic with your hypothesis? What about subject compensation or other recruitment devices? The impact of paying people to respond must be considered. Even a small sum for people in need could affect their responses. It might be better to eliminate these people than to try to compensate for potential bias.

There are a number of sources for obtaining a sample of the population to whom you plan to generalize.

Psychology Classes. One popular source is the human subjects pool in psychology classes. It is common practice to require psych students to take part in a given number of experiments as part of their class assignment.

Here, the obvious question is, "Are respondents who are compelled to participate in an investigation significantly different from those who cooperate of their own free will?" Some psychology departments address this potential bias by giving students a choice between being a subject in a classmate's project or writing a paper on an appropriate subject. Does this eliminate the bias?

To answer this question affirmatively, you would argue that because the option not to participate was available, coercion could be eliminated as a source of bias.

School Children. School children are a favorite target group for dissertation researchers, although getting access to them is likely to require a major effort, perhaps the intervention of a faculty member with public school connections. School kids are fiercely (and properly) protected from the numerous claims on their time since "time-on-task" research showed a significant correlation between uninterrupted study and achievement. This serves to remind us that research does affect what happens in practice.

DATA GATHERING

Having identified what you believe to be a representative or probabilistic sample, you are ready to enter the data-gathering phase of the project. Soon you encounter that researcher's dilemma, missing data. Although you sent out 100 questionnaires, you only got 50 back and a number of these were illegible or had questions not answered. It may surprise you to learn that a 50 percent response rate is considered a good return for a first-time mailing. Nevertheless, you decide to send follow-up questionnaires to all non-responders.

Again, we need to ask whether those who responded the first time are different from those needing a reminder. Comparisons between first and second mailings can be made statistically, of course, but I suggest selecting two samples at the outset with the second at least half again as large as the first. The second sample can be used to replace missing data from the first sample. This procedure eliminates time gaps between mailings and also allows you to replace damaged or illegible information which inevitably occurs with paper and pencil instruments.

How Good are Your Variables?

In addition to the representativeness of the sample, consider the validity of the variables you are using. Perhaps you are studying aggression. Can you assume that aggression means the same thing when exhibited by teenagers in a New York housing development as when it is exhibited by teenagers in a prep school in upstate New York? What will you accept as evidence of aggression? Social science research overflows with slippery terms such as aggression, frustration, motivation, altruism, and other fascinating but hard-to-measure abstractions. Key concepts must be represented in empirical terms, that is, made operational to maximize agreement between judges observing behaviors.

Instrumentation

A large portion of your Method chapter will be devoted to a description of the instruments you plan to use to test your various hypotheses. Present each instrument by name, author, and type (examples of type include achievement tests, attitude scales, criterion-referenced tests, Likert-type scales, questionnaires, and structured interviews). Give information about the purpose of the instrument, the group upon which it was standardized, the number of items it contains, the scoring procedure, and validity and reliability estimates. There are literally thousands of measures to choose from and the advantages of using one with established validity and reliability estimates are many, the most obvious being that you won't have to conduct these estimates for yourself.

Validity

No matter how brilliant your ideas or how well you pose the problem, you are on shaky ground unless you can show reasonable validity and reliability for your instruments. You will remember that validity means the extent to which the test measures what it purports to measure, and reliability means that it measures what it measures consistently.

Validity is not an immutable concept: it depends upon how the instrument is used. Suppose a teacher wants to measure a student's understanding of mathematical principles yet gives a test containing several computational problems. In this case a valid instrument is being used in an invalid manner and the teacher isn't measuring what he or she thinks is being measured. Validity will also be jeopardized if the instrument is used on groups for which it was never intended, perhaps testing adults with a test standardized on children, or assessing immigrants with a test designed for mainstream Americans.

Be sure you understand the three major types of validity: content validity, criterion-referenced validity, and construct validity.

1. Content Validity. Also called face validity, content validity indicates how well the content covers the universe of possible items (questions, true/false statements, math problems), pertaining to the characteristics being measured. Determining content validity involves judgment; does the history test cover all the important events and their implications for the pertinent time period?

Indices of content validity are usually presented descriptively, in the form of percentages of agreement among judges.

2. Criterion-Referenced Validity Versus Norm-Referenced Validity. In distinguishing between these two kinds of validity, we must focus upon the way a subject's performance is evaluated. Instead of comparing an individual's score with others in the same normative group, as in norm-referenced testing, we evaluate his or her performance relative to an "outside" standard either now or in the future. In the "now case," it might be attainment of mastery, defined as responding correctly to a certain number of questions. In the "future case," it might be correctly identifying puppies capable of successfully completing the Seeing Eye program.

Criterion-referenced validity coefficients are an estimate of the relationship between the instrument and the outside criterion. In the above case it would be between the test's predictions and the number of dogs actually becoming Seeing Eye Dogs, e.g., the criterion. Criterion-referenced validity coefficients are generally quite modest, ranging anywhere from .30 to .55.

3. Construct-Validity. Construct validity is an estimate of an instrument's capacity to measure psychological properties. This type of validity is clearly distinguished from other kinds because it is inextricably entwined with theoretical assumptions and meanings. Perhaps you are studying the effect of commitment on perseverance, hypothesizing that the higher your subjects' commitment, the stronger will be their perseverance. Perseverance can be defined operationally in behavioral terms (number of minutes spent on task, for example), but the notion of commitment is a psychological abstraction—a construct which may be *implied*, but not directly *observed*. This is where you bring in theory-based assumptions to explain your choice of variables and to support your hunches about their interrelationships.

Let's use another example to illustrate the importance of underlying theory. An experimental situation is set-up under the assumption that an accumulation of failure experiences will result in cessation of effort for most subjects. Working from a classical behaviorist stimulus/response mode, you might simply observe the number of failure experiences it took before each individual stopped trying, and draw your conclusions from such data.

On the other hand, if you are operating out of attribution theory, you would have to take into consideration the meaning your subjects *attributed* to their failure experiences in order to draw conclusions. The design of the first experiment could safely ignore what was going on in the minds of your subjects. The design of the second one would have to capture this hidden variable.

Reliability

Reliability is somewhat more straightforward because it is never concerned with the meaning of the variables being tested, only with consistency of results. Rubber bands are not as reliable as yardsticks because their flexibility makes it hard to get the same measurement on the same object each time.

Reliability is expressed as a coefficient to indicate the proportion of variance *not* due to errors of measurement. An instrument with a coefficient of .87 tells you that 13 percent of the variance is error variance, and 87 percent is non-error, or "true" variance. As noted in the discussion on sampling error, longer tests tend to be more reliable than shorter tests.

Does this mean that you can continue indefinitely to increase the reliability estimate by adding new items to the instrument? The answer is "no." Lengthening the test runs into the law of diminishing returns. Use the Spearman-Brown formula to indicate how much additional items will raise the reliability estimate. Remember that with each new increment of length, the increased effect on reliability will be less than for the previous increment.[4] Also remember that additional test items must measure the same content and present an equal level of difficulty as those on the original instrument.

Internal Consistency as an Estimate of Reliability. Internal consistency is an estimate of the degree to which the scores on all items on a test intercorrelate. Instead of correlating the first half of a test with the latter half, or odd items with even ones, use the Kuder-Richardson formula which gives you a mean of all possible split-half correlations as an estimate of the instrument's reliability. A big advantage of internal consistency as a measure of reliability is that the test need be administered only once.

An acceptable estimate of internal consistency on a test of approximately 40 items is .80.[5] Should you be dissatisfied with the reliability of your instrument, the Spearman-Brown Formula will tell you how reliability will be affected if you double or triple the number of items on your instrument.

Test-retest as an Estimate of Reliability. Another way to measure reliability is to correlate the scores on a single test administered to the same group of individuals on two separate occasions. The problem with this method is the variety of carry-over effects from one testing situation to another. Some test-takers (but not all), learn from taking the test the first time, and this "practice effect" can impair the reliability estimate. Some test-takers (but not all), remember their responses from the first time and repeat them, perhaps in the interest of consistency. This "memory effect" also interferes with the accuracy of the reliability estimate.

In an attempt to minimize these carry-over effects, some researchers increase the interval between test administrations, but this increases the likelihood that the "true" scores will change over time. Now suppose you construct an additional (parallel) test, keeping the content and level of difficulty as similar as possible to the first one.

Equivalence as an Estimate of Reliability. Your success in designing a new test to parallel the original one will be revealed by the intercorrelations among scores on the two forms. It will eliminate those two demons, practice and memory effects. The primary disadvantage is the time and effort that goes into developing forms that are actually equivalent. Constructing one test that captures the essence of any domain is time-consuming enough, but producing a parallel one may be impractical insofar as time and money are concerned. The surest way to determine the usefulness of a measure for your purposes is to conduct a pilot study.

ADVANTAGES OF A PILOT STUDY

A pilot study can be undertaken to analyze some specific aspect of the investigation, or to look at the efficacy of major hypotheses upon which the entire project rests. "De-bugging" your research design in this way before committing yourself will bring to light potential problems while they still can be corrected without great expenditures of time, money, and effort.

Some faculty routinely require you to conduct a pilot study before they will approve your proposal. This requirement is almost inevitable when you have designed your own measures and have no validity and reliability estimates for them. It is also recommended when you use an established instrument on groups for which it was not intended.

There is no better way to convince a skeptical committee member of the power of a statistical treatment, the sensitivity of a measure, or the merit of a research design, than to present empirical evidence in the form of a pilot study.

Ana Maria, a candidate for a Ph.D. in counseling psychology, wanted to test her assumption that leaderless self-help groups were better at reducing students' test anxiety than those led by licensed psychologists. So great was her personal investment in her hypothesis, that it took two pilot tests to convince her there were no significant differences between these two approaches, at least none that could be detected by her current research design.

Coming to the rescue, Ana Maria's chair suggested adding three more independent variables: substance abuse, weight loss, and depression.

> Although I had to have a house fall on me before I was convinced, I'm sure glad my first two pilots showed no significant differences. By adding those three new independent variables I was able to support my idea that leaderless groups are better, at least for some therapies. My study showed they are better for the treatment of weight loss and depression, and leader-led groups are better for substance abuse. It doesn't seem to make any difference in the treatment of test anxiety.

There was no penalty for failing to support one's hypothesis in Ana Maria's department, and she could have earned her Ph.D. using her first design. If she had, however, she might have always regarded what turned out to be a useful line of investigation as a dead end.

Now, as a faculty member in a department of counselor education, she is using "spin-offs" from her thesis to write a grant application to study leadership styles in non-academic settings.

RESEARCH ETHICS AND THE PROTECTION
OF HUMAN SUBJECTS

If research is to benefit the scientific community and society at large, each researcher must adhere to a strict code of ethics. Knowing Ana Maria as well as I do, I'm sure it never occurred to her to falsify the data simply because her hunch was not coming out "right."

Nonetheless, in both academia and the commercial world, the stakes are high enough to tempt some people to alter findings to support hypotheses. When this happens, everybody suffers—the reputations of universities and the broader scientific community, as well as the consumer who must rely on information from these sources.

Science, in its purist form, is based upon the conviction that finding answers to important questions is worth the effort no matter how the investigation turns out. In some areas students face no pressure for any particular outcome. In education, for example, they are generally free to "search for truth wherever it may lead." However, in the sciences, students often are participants in their advisor's research, projects that could be funded by an outside commercial entity. In such cases, there may very well be economic reasons for obtaining certain outcomes, and pressure to find the "right" answers.

No student should proceed without the review and approval of the Human Subjects Committee or its equivalent. Advisors often fail to tell students not to proceed until their proposals have been reviewed. They often neglect to tell them they need an informed consent agreement to be signed by the subjects in the study. This is a hot button issue, one that can be a potential conflict of interest for the student.

Due to abuse of human subjects in the past in the name of science, academic researchers are required to take steps to protect participants from risk posed by their investigations, whether it be emotional or physical. This includes invasion of privacy, humiliation, risk to reputation, and physical discomfort. For your own self-protection, I suggest giving each person a written statement briefly describing your study, its risks and benefits, and what will be expected of them.

Every university has guidelines to protect human subjects, and most have a committee whose task it is to rule on procedures and adequacy of safeguards. Faculty and student researchers are required to complete a protocol statement before beginning the project. For example, your protocol statement might address the following questions: How will the identity of respondents be kept confidential? Is there a possibility of embarrassing an identifiable group of people? Have the risks and benefits been explained sufficiently and have subjects been notified of their right to withdraw at any time?

With reputations at stake, universities take these matters very seriously. Scholars were formerly free of such constraints and some argue that protection has gone too far, unnecessarily inhibiting the exercise of free inquiry.[6] Be that as it may, an often-used example will serve to illustrate the point.

A landmark experiment on obedience and conformity conducted in 1961 showed subjects willing to administer a series of what they thought were painful shocks to a middle-aged man despite his anguished cries. In reality, no one was *physically* hurt, yet this study would probably be considered abusive and would not be approved today.[7]

Even more to the point is the infamous Tuskegee Syphilis study, conducted in 1932. Several hundred syphilitic black men were enrolled in a program to study the *untreated* effects of syphilis over time. Penicillin was the accepted treatment, yet it was withheld, and subjects were not informed of the danger. Syphilis affects both genders and all ethnic groups, yet only African American men were studied. This project was stopped in 1973, but not before many became seriously ill, transmitted their disease to others or died.

Other Ethical Issues

Students should know the procedures for reporting unethical conduct. If there is fraud, the student is often in a position to find it. There have been instances where a student observes data being altered to achieve a certain result, or witnesses some other unethical practice. This poses an enormous problem. Should he/she risk everything by reporting it? Will the report be kept confidential? What protection is provided for the student? The answers, of course, depend upon the particular circumstances. Fortunately, these occasions are rare and most universities offer some kind of protection for "whistle-blowers."

Authorship Issues

Suppose a student is working with an advisor on a project and expects to use his/her share of the research in his dissertation. Who owns the data? Who should be the first author if the investigation is published? There have been cases in which the professor claims that the student took "his" data and published it as his own. The student argues that he/she did the research on that part of the project and had every right to have it published.

In fact, the professor owns the basic data and the student owns the dissertation. but untangling one from the other can be difficult. These questions, along with who should be first author in case the work is published should be addressed and agreed upon at the outset.

WRITING STYLE

University departments and graduate divisions require doctoral candidates to follow a specific style manual in reporting their research findings. Your advisor, your department, or the graduate division of your university will have manuals recommended for your particular discipline.

Follow this manual from the very outset so each footnote, quotation, reference, table, figure, and heading in your notes and rough drafts will not require changing into the proper format later. By the time you write the final draft these conventions will be ingrained in your consciousness, leaving you free to concentrate on more substantive matters.

The majority of dissertations are scientific reports, written in a technical style. This is not to say that imagination and conjecture have no place. Imagination enlivens and enriches both the process and the outcome. Conjecture is the basis of theory-building and a vehicle for travel into uncharted waters. When you venture beyond your data, however, be sure to make it clear that you are deliberately leaving the solid ground of evidence-supported findings to enter the realm of speculation.

The style in which findings are reported must meet high standards of logic, organization, and clarity. Flights of pure fancy, unsupported opinions, sweeping generalizations, and proselytizing do not belong in technical writing.

Students in the social sciences have been given this warning so often, and are so leery of sounding unscientific, that they may go to the other extreme, embracing a style that is stilted, pedantic, and unnatural. This has been labeled "dissertationspeak."

In dissertationspeak, the tone is apologetic and defensive, intended more to protect the writer against the aggressive queries of the committee than to communicate with the reader. Such tendencies make it nearly impossible to convert dissertations into books without extensive rewriting. University press editors, who receive manuscripts based upon dissertations, note that writers are plagued by servility to their committees, and seem to be convinced that every statement must be substantiated by a "cowardly conditional." Parsons gives this shining example of defensive writing:

> All things else being equal, it would appear to be the case that, under given circumstances, it may not be uncommon for writers of dissertations to execute certain prose styles which those who seem to like their English straight and strong might conceivably call a perversion of the languages.[8]

The line between "insider language" and "English straight and strong" is, of course, a matter of judgment. The best course is to write to the educated layperson, using enough of the terminology of your discipline to show that you speak the language, yet not so much that you sound as if you were deliberately spouting jargon.

By the time you write the Results section of your research, you will be so familiar with every aspect of it that you may have unwittingly omitted important points or given explanations that don't explain. At this juncture, a professional editor is worth his or her weight in gold. If your budget is down to pennies by this time, try to find an educated layperson to read your proposal for understandability as well as for grammatical and typographical errors.

THE PROPOSAL HEARING

After attending to everybody's concerns in one way or another (strictly following some ideas and negotiating others), you finally have the latest, and you hope, final draft of your proposal and are ready to seek the endorsement of the committee as a whole.

Ask the department secretary how to go about scheduling a hearing and what paperwork is required. Make certain to obtain the necessary signatures, submit the proper papers, and check all deadlines. You may think this is too obvious to mention, but it is amazing how many otherwise conscientious students are sloppy about such routine matters!

At this formal hearing all committee members will have a chance to put in their final two cents worth before agreeing you are ready to begin your investigation. It may be the first and only time you see your committee together in one place before the oral defense of the thesis. You can use the occasion to pick up valuable insights into the ways they interact as a group.

The Hearing as a Trial Run for the Defense

Think of this hearing as a trial run for the final oral and be sure that your chair "hears" everything you did, both overt and implied. This is a test of the working relationship between the two of you. Remember Tom's experience described in Chapter 1? His chair was trying to throw him a life line and he failed to recognize it.

Be alert to matters of personality as well as matters of substance. As a student, you are in no position to ameliorate personality clashes among faculty members, but simply knowing where the coalitions and antagonisms lie helps you read the political climate.

Expect an Adversarial Relationship

Recognize that you and the institution stand in an *adversarial* relationship insofar as defending the proposal is concerned. The same conditions will prevail when you defend your dissertation. You are there as an advocate of your plan and the committee is there in a gate-keeping capacity, representing the department and university.

This shouldn't make you unduly defensive because, in the long run, the committee is on your side. Criticisms and suggestions are intended to improve the project, not to trip you up or embarrass you. While no one wants you to fail, they would rather have you fail than accept an inadequate piece of work which embarrasses them and the university. It is understandable and acceptable to show some nervousness. As a matter of fact, self-confidence which borders on arrogance can elicit more aggressive questioning than would otherwise be the case.

The best preparation is to play devil's advocate with your own work throughout each stage in its development. Form a habit of taking the role of an adversary who is actively looking for inconsistencies, omissions, poorly reasoned arguments, overblown generalizations, and illogical conclusions. Ask yourself what alternative explanations might be found to explain those findings equally well.

Never try to defend the indefensible. When weaknesses in your study are revealed, it is better to acknowledge them and suggest (or ask for) ways to strengthen or change them. Even better, *briefly* point out weaknesses before others do. Don't dwell on them, don't cover them up, and don't apologize. Pointing out weaknesses in one's work is not only honest, it displays the kind of self-correcting attitudes that are fundamental to good research.

In a high pressure situation, it is easy to misunderstand questions put to you. Unless you are certain you understand the question, follow the time-honored advice to pause, take a sip of water, and rephrase the question in your own words. This isn't the mark of an amateur, but of a professional who is accustomed to fielding questions. Immediately after the hearing, write down all directives and suggestions and verify them with your chair as soon as possible.

Occasionally, one of the examiners may seem intent on pursuing an insignificant or even unjustified point beyond what seems reasonable. When this happens, it is a good guess that the examiner is trying to impress his or her colleagues. There are two ways to handle the situation: you can stand your ground and argue logically and *non-defensively* for your position, or you can appear to accept the suggestion while resolving to consider it at greater length later on, perhaps under the aegis of your chair or a sympathetic committee member. Whatever you do, keep in mind that your goal is to walk out of that room with an approved proposal in hand, even one with conditions attached.

Congratulations! You are now ready to move into the action phase of your quest. Modifications notwithstanding, you have passed a major milestone on your way to the doctorate. The doubts and ambiguities that troubled you up to this point have been greatly reduced. Faculty approval of your proposal is a strong vote of confidence that you have the ability and the will to complete the job. It is an occasion for celebration so find a way to reward yourself.

SUMMARY

Having an approved proposal is a pledge that the faculty and the university will keep their part of the bargain. This is about as close as you can get to a written contract and is one of the few safeguards in the uncertain world of doctoral study. It provides continuity in case a faculty member leaves and offers some protection against a disinterested or even hostile committee member. It gives you experience in grant-writing (with expert critics), a survival skill you will need as a junior faculty member, striving to bring in "soft" money to support your research. The most immediate and most pragmatic reason for writing a proposal is that it will translate relatively easily into the first three chapters of your dissertation—a time saver in the long run.

The current trend in social science dissertations is toward shorter, "meatier," dissertations, closer to journal style than the book-length productions of previous years. Some sponsors urge their students to include only the most germane references in the literature review and to postpone working on this section until after the empirical part of the investigation is complete. Only upon completion of the research, they argue, is it possible to determine which references are pertinent and which are peripheral.

To provide a brief refresher in research terminology and a guide for writing the Methods chapter, I defined and illustrated some basic statistical concepts. A particularly useful one for social scientists is "disproportionate sampling," a technique for making inferences from sample groups which differ widely in the number of individuals they represent.

The proposal hearing is arguably *the* major hurdle in the long road to the doctorate. In this chapter I try to put it into perspective and suggest ways to prepare for it. Playing devil's advocate with one's own work is a habit that should be cultivated; it will yield a lifetime of benefits. Every suggestion for change doesn't have to be followed verbatim, however, you may argue *non-defensively* against some and appear to accept others while making a mental reservation to discuss their merit with your chair. Be willing to negotiate minor modifications in your plan, but whatever strategy you follow, remember that your goal is to walk out of the hearing with an approved proposal.

NOTES

1. Madsen, David: *Successful Dissertations and Theses: A Guide to Graduate Student Research from Proposal to Completion.* San Francisco, Jossey-Bass, 1983.
2. Yates is writing especially for Ph.D. candidates in psychology, but his advice is good for other disciplines as well. He cautions that, in addition to diverting students from the empirical investigation, comprehensive reviews take months to put together. Yates, Brian T.: *Doing the Dissertation: The Nuts and Bolts of Psychological Research.* Springfield, IL, Charles C Thomas, 1982.
3. This is a particularly good book for students because it clearly demonstrates the value of analyses which avoid type II errors. Kraemer, Helen C. & Thiemann, Sue: *How Many Subjects: Statistical Power Analysis in Research.* Newbury Park, Sage, 1987.
4. Lemke, E. and Wiersma, W.: *Principles of Psychological Measurement.* Boston, Houghton Mifflin, 1976, p. 87.
5. Long, Thomas J., Convey, JJ., and Chwalek, A.R.: *Completing Dissertations in the Behavioral Sciences and Education.* San Francisco, Jossey-Bass, 1985.
6. Oversight committees have to balance the scientific value of an experiment with the well-being of human subjects, and in borderline cases this is often a difficult judgement call. See de Sola Pool, I.: The new censorship of social research. *Public Interest,* 59:57-66, 1980.
7. Clearly, Milgram's study has had an impact on education and clinical practice and is still cited despite the fact that over 40 years have elapsed since its publication. Milgram, S.: Some conditions of obedience and disobedience to authority. In Steiner and Fishbein (Eds): *Current Studies in Social Psychology.* New York, Holt, Rinehart & Winston, 1965.
8. Parsons, P.: *Getting Published: The Acquisition Process at University Presses.* Knoxville, University of Tennessee Press, 1989.

Chapter 6

THE DISSERTATION

This is your moment of truth. You are about to put your plan into operation, to test your hunches, and lay your formal hypotheses on the line. Before getting down to the nitty gritty of data collection and analysis, however, let us consider some of the conditions that support or impede your efforts. We will start with that most precious of commodities, *time.*

TIME, THE IRREPLACEABLE RESOURCE

Guard your time more carefully than you guard your wallet. Once it has slipped away, it is harder to recoup than money. Allocate prime time, the hours when your brain is at its best, to the most important jobs and leave low-energy periods for the "no-brainer" jobs. The schedule that worked best for me was from four in the morning to the middle of the afternoon five days per week. During the quiet early morning hours I found the solitude I needed for creative thinking and energy for exacting tasks. My creativity level diminished rapidly after lunch so I used afternoons to record data, check references, and perform other mundane tasks.

If you are more of an owl than a lark, this schedule may not fit you at all. As an undergraduate, you might have developed a habit of waiting until after dinner to settle down to serious study which continued into the small hours of the morning. With the added burden of home and family responsibilities, however, some students find themselves beginning to act more like owls. I have noticed this change of life style especially with parents of small children. Work schedules seem to be most productive when they coincide, to some extent, with times when most of the rest of the world is asleep.

Paid Employment in Addition to Doctoral Pursuit?

The subject of scheduling inevitably brings up the wisdom of holding down a job while simultaneously pursuing a Ph.D. I can only repeat the advice you have probably already heard: it is worth almost any sacrifice (short of the threat of starvation) to devote yourself full time to your studies. Students with family responsibilities often hesitate to ask spouses and children to make sacrifices, yet most families are willing to endure a few years of delayed gratification when they recognize the potential of the degree to benefit the entire family unit. Even children are proud that Mom or Dad goes to school just like they do!

For some who can't afford full time student-hood, part-time employment is another option, especially if the work is dissertation-related.

Becoming a teaching or research assistant (TA or RA), or securing a funded research grant doesn't pay very much, but it may bring in enough money to ward off starvation. I hasten to add, however, that not every TA and RA experience works out well for the student. Note these cautionary words of Allison, a student about to conclude an unusually successful experience as a research assistant.

I was so thrilled when Dr. M asked me to be her RA that I said "yes" quickly before she could change her mind. All I could think of was what a great opportunity this was and how pleased Bill would be with the additional income. I didn't stop to worry that my arrangement was oral and very casual.

Eight months have gone by and I'm still happy with the arrangement. Despite long hours and short pay, I've learned a lot about research that I have been able to apply to my dissertation.

It was only when I listened to other RAs and TAs that I realized I had really lucked out with Dr. M. I heard about horrible experiences of other assistants, like being forced to run labs which took twice as long as the classes they'd originally agreed to teach and I heard about profs who demanded so much (especially during finals) that the TA's own work suffered terribly. One person said that being a TA set him back a whole year and it wasn't worth the pittance it paid.

Knowing what I know now, I'd advise others to have a written contract and check with other students who had worked for this prof before signing on as an assistant.

Time-to-Degree and the Probability of Finishing

An inverse relationship seems to exist between the time it takes students to finish and the probability that they will complete their studies and eventually capture the Ph.D. Exceptions to this generality notwithstanding, the axiom in academic circles is that as the years spent in pursuit of the doctorate *increase*, the chances of finishing *decrease*.

Remember Michael in Chapter 1 whose interview was going well until the search committee realized he had been "All But Dissertation" for nearly four years? His ABD status was a red flag signaling that he was an employment risk. Departments don't want to be saddled with profs who are unlikely to move beyond the assistant professor's rank. They tend to believe that slow-moving students will become slow-moving profs. One way to keep yourself on the move is to set a schedule and move heaven and earth to live up to it.

The Importance of Following a Schedule

However you arrange your schedule, reserve a *minimum* of four hours a day for uninterrupted study, six to eight hours are better if you can swing it. The point of diminishing returns appears somewhere between six and eight hours for most people; then they begin to spin their wheels, or even worse, to make costly mistakes. Make sure your schedule fits your energy level, the time reasonably available to you, and your own unique lifestyle.

Once established, do whatever it takes to stick to the schedule. You might want to put a "Do Not Disturb" sign on your door. Hang in there even during those times when your brain seems out to lunch. Don't let yourself off the hook during those inevitable periods when you are not at your intellectual peak. Postpone demanding tasks in favor of routine ones, but keep on working. The goal is to establish a mind/body routine that will become habitual. Not only do you train yourself by doing so, you put spouses, lovers, family, and friends on notice that your study time is sacrosanct. Writing a dissertation is not the kind of undertaking you can put down and pick up again without losing continuity and forward momentum. Two hours in the morning, one hour in the afternoon, and one hour after dinner may add up to four *arithmetically*, but time divided is seldom as fruitful as four consecutive hours of concentrated effort. Each interruption breaks your train of thought and makes you struggle to gear up and regain forward motion. Your mind, like your computer, needs a certain amount of time to "load the software."

The Importance of Changing the Pace

Computers don't go stale but humans beings really do, so treat yourself to short periods away from your work. Make time off count by engaging in activities as opposite as possible from your scholarly routine. Vigorous physical exercise is a pleasant contrast to hours spent hunched over a book or glued to the monitor.

Your spirit needs refreshing too. Try to squeeze in quality time with loved ones. Supportive others provide a life line to the outside world and help you keep ivory tower problems in perspective. Whomever you see, avoid people (even family members) who drag you down through insensitivity to your task or outright jealousy. Whether failing to understand your endeavor or openly antagonistic to it, people like this sap your enthusiasm and diminish your self confidence. Who needs them?

The Importance of Time for Reflection

To be a disciplined scholar you don't have to go about your work with grim determination. In fact, the thing that makes research so interesting is that it calls for a wide variety of approaches, some focused and tightly controlled, and others playful, imaginative, and unfettered. You can't force creativity; that is an oxymoron. Innovative ideas as well as solutions to perplexing problems are as likely to appear out of the blue when you are in a relaxed state of mind as when you are in hot pursuit of an idea or solution. Good schedules are those that build in time to reflect, as Lydia, a candidate for a Ph.D. in linguistics finally came to realize.

Lydia seemed to have everything going for her. A distinguished scholar in the linguistics department at a prestigious Midwestern university had agreed to chair her committee and gave her an assistantship. She had an approved proposal and was well launched into the implementation phase of her dissertation when she ran into difficulties that wouldn't yield to her usual method of handling problems.

> Things have been going so well, but lately everything's been falling apart: my work, my relationship with Dr. J., and even my love life! I keep thinking of that old saying from *Alice in Wonderland,* "The hurrieder I go, the behinder I get."[1]

> I even *feel* like Alice. I'm in a looking-glass world where nothing makes sense. Every hoop I jump is followed by another one and the hoops keep getting higher and faster. Last night I broke up with my boyfriend and this morning Dr. J said the statistics "didn't support my inferences about social distance and linguistic behavior for at least half of my ethnic groups. I wanted to talk about these results, but he cut me short and rushed off to a meeting.

As an undergraduate, Lydia did everything as fast as possible. She thought fast, she talked fast, she even walked fast, and prided herself on always being among the first to finish an exam and leave the room.

Now, as a Ph.D. candidate, the stakes were higher and she was even more goal-oriented, convinced any obstacle could be surmounted by sheer determination and hard work. She never bothered to join the student network and had more than once offended the department secretary by her blunt manner.

After thinking it through, Lydia realized her usual plan of attack wasn't working. She sought help at the university counseling center and gradually came to understand that driving herself so unmercifully was not only bad for her mental health, it also brought her intellectual efforts to a halt. Although she remained a somewhat tense, overachiever, Lydia learned how important it was to let the goal dictate the approach. Some goals are reached through highly concentrated directed effort and others by letting ideas soak and percolate in consciousness.

CONDUCTING YOUR INVESTIGATION

After all that planning, it is time for action. Whether you are analyzing questionnaires or deciphering manuscripts written in Assyrian cuneiform, the challenge is to retrieve your data and organize them in a manner compatible with your research problem.

Become Familiar With Your Data

A statistician friend of mine recommends that all researchers enter their own data in the computer, even if they can afford to hire an assistant for this exacting and time-consuming task. Simply being in intimate contact with data in their raw form helps you see if there is anything "funny" going on with your numbers. Take a look at the descriptive statistics included in most statistical packages which portray your data in graphic form. Look at scatter plots, frequency distributions, means, medians, modes, standard deviations, skewness, and kurtosis (the degree of "peakedness" in the distribution). Look for large gaps in the sequence of numerical data, for curvilinearity (see Table 1, Chapter 5), and for "outliers," those few scores that fall far outside the distribution. Make it your business to know if there is a pile-up of scores at one point, and if there are no cases between the scores of 65 and 80. The end products: correlations, *f ratios*, *t* scores, and factor loadings don't tell the whole story. There is something *heuristic* about working with raw data that can be acquired no other way. This reminds me of the delightful older lady in E. M. Forster's *Aspects of the Novel*, who, when accused of being illogical, replied, "Logic? Good gracious! What rubbish! How can I tell what I think 'till I see what I say?"

This is as good a definition of heuristic as any I have ever heard.

Becoming familiar with your data doesn't mean you should always conduct your own measurements. Especially in experimental studies, simply knowing how you *want* people to react, risks shaping their behavior and contaminating the results. It isn't worth the risk. If there is even a remote possibility of introducing bias through "telegraphing" your intentions, it is better to train others to run your experiments. Then you won't find yourself explaining to examiners at your oral defense how careful you were to avoid influencing outcomes. Your procedures will speak for you.

Because research assistants play such a crucial role in the quality of the data, give considerable thought to the selection of people to run experiments, administer tests, conduct interviews, or otherwise collect information. Careful selection, followed by equally careful training and management in process, will give you confidence in your data base. A shaky foundation (sometimes called "dirty data") contaminates the results and threatens the whole enterprise.

A written script explaining exactly what is expected of your data-gatherers will help to ensure consistency among them. Clearly, these people are a kind of stimuli in and of themselves, so it is important to standardize their influence (hold it constant) to the extent possible. A good training device is to have them take turns role-playing both the subject and the interviewer. Training sessions should also include practice in scoring and recording subjects' responses in proper form.

You may not need research assistants if you are using self-administering instruments mailed to respondents' homes or otherwise presented to them with accompanying written or computer-aided instructions. A pilot study will tell you whether instructions are understandable to people who are roughly equivalent to the group you plan to test.

Tips to Help Increase Return Rates of Mailed Questionnaires

As noted in the previous chapter, a 50 percent response for mailed questionnaires is considered adequate. Unfortunately, many rates of return are much lower than that, and of course, you want as high a percentage return rate as you can get. Some of my colleagues have been successful in designing measures and cover letters that elicit a high rate of return. These are some of their suggestions:

1. Address respondents by name, if at all possible, not dear friend, student, sir, madame, or occupant.
2. Use first class mail.
3. Send a *brief* but *persuasive*, cover letter outlining the importance of the study.
4. Send a small amount of money with the questionnaire to increase a sense of obligation.
5. Avoid complex sentences and dense text. Leave lots of white spaces surrounding print.
7. Send follow-up postcards one week later to non-responders.
8. Send a follow-up letter with a replacement questionnaire to non-responders three weeks after mailing the postcards.
9. Send a letter with replacement questionnaire to non-respondents by certified mail six weeks after that.

It is up to you to choose among these suggestions for those that fit your research, your schedule, and your pocketbook.

More expensive in time and money, and certainly not self-administering, are a couple of other data-gathering techniques, the personal interview and the telephone survey.

The Personal Interview

Personal interviews have several advantages. For one thing, they permit the interviewer to correct any misunderstandings and erroneous interpretations the respondent might have about the inquiry, and provide opportunities to pick up clues about the respondent and his/her environment which can help in the interpretation of results. For another, spontaneous oral answers tend to be more truthful than written ones where people have time to consider their answers. Finally, face-to-face interviews guarantee that responses come from the intended subject instead of from some other person who might have completed the questionnaire in the respondent's place.

A major disadvantage of personal interviews is the cost. Reimbursing interviewers for their time and travel present formidable financial obstacles for many graduate students. Moreover, unless interviewers are exceptionally well trained, the resulting data can be incomplete and even misleading. A final disadvantage worth considering is that many people are afraid to admit strangers to their homes without an introductory letter or phone call.

Telephone Interviews

Estimates have shown that telephone surveys can be made for 45 percent to 65 percent of the cost of personal interviews and that the response rate for phone interviews exceeds that of mail surveys by some 17 percentage points.[2]

Disadvantages of this sampling method include the fact that Americans are becoming increasingly impatient with dinnertime and television-viewing-time interruptions, yet the evening hours are precisely the time to catch people at home. In contrast to face-to-face interviews, it is very easy to say, "not interested," and hang up the phone. Moreover, we know very little about how long people are willing to talk or what techniques elicit the most truthful answers. We do know that the caller must quickly establish credibility and pique the respondent's interest or lose the listener. Pollster Oscar Kaplan sums up the drawbacks of telephone interviews: "Answering machines, unlisted numbers, and an increasing refusal rate are making it more difficult to obtain a true random sample by telephone."[3]

Some researchers recommend, and some research designs require, a combination of mailed or telephoned introductory contacts followed by face-to-face interviews. This may be the best of all possible worlds if you can afford it.

It is tempting to use a statistical procedure without thoroughly understanding it, because of the ease with which you can plug in numbers and let the computer do your thinking for you. How can you choose among options when you have only a hazy idea of the distinctions among them? Suppose you are trying to find the best predictors of success in college among several variables: high school grades, SAT scores, parents' educational level, and the quality of the student's application essay. The order in which these variables are entered in a regression equation affects the results; should you use a forward, backward, or stepwise strategy? If you don't change the order to suit your purposes, the person who designed the software will make the decision for you, *by default.* Options to override the default are used to decide when to terminate iterations in an iterative analysis, how many factors to rotate in factor analysis, and which test to use among several in a multivariate analysis of variance. Just as you don't want to abdicate your decision-making power to a consultant who is somewhat familiar with the data, you don't want to let a software author who has never seen your study shape the results. Poorly planned use of computer technology quickly catches up with you when you try to interpret the results.

Data for Entry into the Computer

We are fortunate that computers have made our lives so much easier in regard to gathering, sorting and processing information.

Spreadsheets using a variety of programs like Excel, mean we no longer have to use numeric codes. Demographic information about your sample needs to be imputed often in the form of independent variables such as gender, race, and socioeconomic status. Age can be recorded in months or years or you might want to include age groups

(21 years to 40, 41 to 50, 51 to 60 years). Examples of other independent variables are: individual identification, group membership, and such control variables as treatment/no treatment, pass/fail, personality type, or grade level. Because the computer can sort the information in a variety of ways, you are no longer restricted to choosing one way to present the information.

A simple research problem will be helpful here. Suppose you're trying to determine the extent to which factual knowledge of healthful practices translates into actual behavior in daily life. Simply put, you are looking for relationships between *knowing* and *doing*. Moreover, your experience suggests there may be some important age, gender, and income differences in the way people apply cognitive knowledge to daily activities. The first order of business is to construct a master data sheet which lists each variable. In our example testing the relationship between cognitive knowledge and daily practice, there are *four* independent variables: gender, age, education, and income, and two dependent variables, (1) respondents' knowledge of good health practices, and (2) the extent to which they report that they put this knowledge into practice. Table II illustrates how the variable names and value labels might be constructed with an example of data sorted by education.

Table II*
VARIABLE NAMES AND VALUE LABELS

Col	*Variable*	*Value Labels*
1	Subject ID	6-digit number
2	Gender	1 = male, 2 = female
3	Age	Age of subject in years (20 to 81 plus)
4	Education	1 = less than high school
		2 = high school diploma
		3 = some college
		4 = college degree
		5 = some graduate education
		6 = graduate degree
5	Income	1 = less than $20,000
		2 = $20,001 to $30,000
		3 = $30,001 to $40,000
		4 = $40,001 to $50,000
		5 = $50,001 to $60,000
		6 = $60,001 to $70,000
		7 = $70,001 and beyond

Table II* (cont.)

Col	Variable	Value Labels
6	Respondents' knowledge of good health practices	1= excellent 2 = good 3 = average 4 = below average 5 = poor
7	Extent to which respondents report putting knowledge into practice	1= excellent 2 = good 3 = average 4 = below average 5 = poor

Table IIa
DATA SORTED BY EDUCATION

NAME or ID#	GENDER	AGE	EDUCATION	INCOME	KNOWLEDGE	PRACTICE
907001	1	20	2	3	4	4
907022	2	30	4	6	1	2
907036	1	25	4	2	3	3
907038	2	48	4	5	2	1
907023	1	50	5	3	2	1
907039	2	77	6	7	1	1
907041	1	44	6	6	2	2

* Table designs by Patricia Frischer and Darwin Slindee.

Missing Values

Every researcher encounters missing values for a variety of reasons. Some responses are illegible, some answers are unknown by the respondent or simply overlooked, and others are deliberately left blank by those who may see them as racist or an invasion of privacy. All computer programs handle unequal sample and cell sizes today, so missing values are not the problem they used to be.

DATA MANAGEMENT

There are three cardinal rules of research.

1. Back up your work, back up your work, *back up your work.* You will need some way at the end of each work day to make a complete copy of your work preferably stored independently. Even though you have automatic back-up, never leave the computer without backing up data on a disk or external hard drive. It may be that everyone needs one bitter experience to become fully convinced of the importance of this rule. I learned it years ago when a grant proposal I was working on disappeared into cyber space two days before it was due. Of course, you also need to save your work during the course of a day. A good habit to acquire is to click on "save" every few minutes.
2. Keep names, social security numbers, or other means of identifying subjects in a safe place away from other data. Enter only ID numbers on the master data file and in the computer.
3. Collect and enter all relevant data while you have the chance, even though several may be discarded later. It is frustrating to find that you have overlooked a variable you thought was insignificant at the time, one that could have been easily captured. Should you decide not to use it, a simple format statement will tell the computer to ignore it.

COMMON DIFFICULTIES AND WHAT TO DO ABOUT THEM

Subject Dropouts

In the realistic anticipation of losing subjects, it is a good strategy to select more subjects than are statistically necessary. In the previous chapter, I noted that there is likely to be at least a 50 percent mortality rate on mailed questionnaires and suggested you plan for this eventuality by doubling the number needed for your analysis. While the dropout rates for investigations where data are collected in face-to-face situations does not usually approach the 50 percent mark, the same principle applies. There are two ways to approach this potential difficulty, by testing more subjects than you expect to wind up with, or by arranging for standbys to replace those who fall by the wayside. Standbys can replace dropouts in basic research projects only when this doesn't violate the statistical assumptions underlying the analysis.

Some advisors go so far as to recommend using dropout status as a *dependent variable* in applied studies, especially when the number of dropouts is sizable. Failure to complete the treatment has implications for practice and can be viewed as a result in itself, helping you turn a potential disaster into an advantage.[4]

A good example of such a "useful" disaster arose near the end of my data-gathering tour. I was at lunch with a group of professors and we were discussing the kinds of catastrophes that can befall the unwary Ph.D. student. A woman from the business school recounted her experience as a young doctoral student, trying to construct a scale to measure what business students thought of female CEOs.

> I was doing a pilot study to get validity and reliability estimates on an instrument I had designed to measure both womens' and mens' perceptions of female CEOs. I had engaged three women assistants to present several fictional case histories to a pool of subjects and to record their perceptions of the ability of these imaginary CEOs on my scale.
>
> The problem was, we kept losing most of our male subjects! The women were intrigued, but some of the men would come once and we'd never see them again. My advisor suggested adding male presenters, and this helped some, but not enough.
>
> It wasn't until I asked a couple of male friends to listen to the presentations that I found out what was wrong. I had inadvertently picked one assistant who was openly antagonistic to men, especially young men. Rather than coming to me to complain, they simply dropped out of the study.
>
> Although I had to let her go, my assistant really did me a big favor. I needed to revise my questionnaire. I located as many of the dropouts as I could find and, with their help, revised my scale to include new items describing women's behaviors that were particularly distasteful to men. The revised questionnaire discriminated well between women likely to be successful CEOs and those who would not.

While my colleague didn't make dropouts a dependent variable, as suggested above, she didn't ignore it either. Instead of trying to solve the problem by continually adding male subjects to the pool until she had sufficient numbers (which would have introduced bias), she took time to find out the reason so many men wanted out. Good researchers learn to be alert to what the data and events are trying to tell them. However you decide to treat a dropout problem once your research is underway, be sure to clear any change in procedures with your chair.

Unsupported Hypotheses

To begin with, remember that you are not seeking to *prove* a theory or hypothesis—only to support or reject a theory or hypothesis within a certain level of probability. The null hypothesis states that there is *zero* relationship between two variables. For example, if you expect to find a relationship between fetal alcohol syndrome and the attention span of infants, you would phrase it negatively: "Fetal alcohol syndrome has no effect on the attention span of infants between the ages of six months and one year of age." Should you fail in your efforts to reject this hypothesis, you cannot claim to have disproved a theory or even that these variables are related. All you can say is that you didn't find statistical evidence to reject the null.

Now, let us assume you *do* find a relationship at the .05 level of probability. This means that the effect of fetal alcohol syndrome on infants' attention span is *not nil*, nothing more. This is a difficult concept to understand, much less accept. No matter how clearly the textbooks and statistics instructors try to correct misconceptions about probability levels, you read reports (even in respected journals) that imply that the statistical term, *significant,* means what it means in everyday language, that is, *vital, important, weighty* or *large.* Extending this line of thinking even farther, are inferences that p $<$.001 is more significant than p $<$.01.[5]

Understandably, you hope to find support for all of your hypotheses and are disappointed when the evidence is not forthcoming. Before deciding that you are on the wrong track, however, I suggest the following:

1. Reexamine the theoretical framework underlying each hypothesis. How well did your research design accommodate the assumptions of the theory? Are there design changes you can still make to probe relationships between and among variables?
2. Were the measurement instruments up to the task you put them to? Lack of construct validity is a common reason for unsubstantiated hypotheses.
3. Did you leave out an important independent variable because you assumed it wasn't relevant to your sample?
4. Did you control properly for co-variates which might have affected the outcome?
5. Do the data show any surprises in the form of limited range, exceptional skewness, too many outliers, or unexpectedly low correlations?
6. Was your treatment or equipment ineffective in some way? Perhaps some participants failed to fully understand what was

expected of them or you didn't allow time for everyone to reach a common level of expertise in operating equipment.

7. How confident are you that your sample is truly representative of the population to which you want to generalize?

Most advisors will encourage you to pursue serendipitous findings and additional clues in the data, even if such new directions were not anticipated in the original proposal. Subsequent analyses are undertaken to examine anomalies in the data, or to understand why support for hypotheses was not found. Sometimes it helps to collapse independent variables into composites and test them against dependent variables. Occasionally, minor variables produce stronger effects than major variables, and the focus of the investigation can be shifted accordingly.

Now, let us pose an extremely unlikely scenario. What if you carefully adhered to *all* the assumptions required by your statistical analyses, checked for errors of omission or commission, and tested all promising relationships, yet still cannot find support for your thesis?

The first thing to realize is that very few investigation find support for all hypotheses and you are under no obligation to have your hunches turn out as expected. Testing a theory, pursuing an idea born of experience, or following a lead in the literature are reasons enough to launch an investigation. Unsupported hypotheses are worth something in their own right and make a contribution to the field if only by saving someone else from pursuing the same rainbow. Unless you are working with an advisor who is under contract with some commercial enterprise (see page 100 under "Research Ethics and the Protection of Human Subjects") your only obligation is to design and conduct the best research project of which you are capable. You need to explain your rationale for doing what you did, and completely and honestly report your findings.

That Ubiquitous Type I Error

Students worry about not finding statistical support for their hypotheses, but a far more common difficulty tends to be overlooked—the pervasiveness of the Type I error—of falsely rejecting the null hypothesis. Type II error, you will recall, is the reverse, the error of accepting the null when it is actually false.

Cohen comments on the ubiquitousness of the Type I Error and widespread misuse of statistics in general. "I have encountered too many studies with prodigious numbers of dependent variables, or with what seemed to me far too many independent variables, or (heaven help us) both." He goes on to say, "Using the .05 level for many tests escalates the experiment wise Type I error rate—or, in plain English, greatly increases the chances of discovering things that aren't so."

By way of illustration, Cohen considers a test of relationships between pairs of six dependent and ten independent variables at p $<$.05 level of significance where the analysis yields six significant relationships out of these 60 tests, (6 dependent by 10 independent variables). Among these six, one could expect an average of *three* spuriously significant ones. This brings up some embarrassing questions, such as, "Well, which three are real?" Or even, "Is six *significantly* more than the chance-expected three?" (it so happens that it isn't).[6]

Unless you are conducting an explicitly exploratory study, I suggest you cull your list of potential variables for those few that show real promise. A pilot test will help distinguish between "promising" and "dead-end" variables. In addition, be cautious about using that overworked p $<$.05 cutoff point to support your argument of a significant relationship among or between variables. A single study, even with significance levels of p $<$.001, does little more than add some weight to one side of an argument. The importance of hedging your bets with *modest* claims will be further discussed in the Conclusions section.

DISSERTATIONS USING QUALITATIVE METHODS

In departments where the orientation is strongly focused on empirical research, there is often a bias against non-quantitative methodologies. This is particularly true in disciplines having strong ties to the medical profession.

Delbert had just finished his course work in speech pathology and was intrigued by the psychological implications of childhood articulation problems that he thought he would investigate, using qualitative methods.

By the expression on Dr. R's face when I suggested a couple of qualitative research methods you'd have thought I was talking about experimenting on kids with hallucinogenics!

He was so put off by my suggestions that I don't think he'd give me a second chance, even if I agreed to go quantitative all the way. I've lost him as an advisor and probably even as a committee member.

After several turndowns from other faculty, I found a newly hired professor who is willing to work with me if I will use both qualitative and quantitative methodologies. It worries me a little that she doesn't have tenure yet, but I think she will get it because of her good publication record. Now I'm concerned that Dr. R will show up at my orals, make me justify my use of ethnographic measures, and generally give me a bad time.

Because it is still the preferred way of analyzing data in many settings, I have emphasized quantitative methods in this chapter and the previous one. Yet not every dissertation deals primarily with numerical data, and some dissertations don't use numbers at all.

Many researchers are challenging experimental and quasi-experimental designs, viewing them as artificial and inflexible. Challenges to traditional methods of inquiry come under various headings such as phenomenology, ethnographic inquiry, representative case method, systematic analysis of interview data, grounded theory research, and descriptive observations. These techniques have been gaining new respectability in the social sciences, although some have been used for years in the humanities. Some researchers combine qualitative and quantitative methods.

Over the past 50 years, behavioral scientists have clung somewhat uncritically to the models and methods of the physical scientists. This pattern continues despite the fact that we know people, unlike algae, do not react predictably to environmental stimuli. Instead, they *interact unpredictably* with environmental stimuli, both shaping and being shaped by the world around them. Attempting to set up "context free" laboratory experiments, in which "objectivity" means the experience is distinct from life experiences, can be like trying to understand a flowing river from a bucket of river water.

Psychologist, William Bevan, urges colleagues to assume a far less rigid, more pragmatic view of what scientists may or may not do. He calls for new intellectual models in the social and behavioral sciences:

> First of all, ask yourself what the essential questions to be answered are, and then ask yourself what you have to do to reach answers that

will convince you and others of the validity of the ideas behind them. Second, be wary of rule-bound methodology. Use any method with a full understanding of what it does for you but also what constraints it may place on you, and whether it violates assumptions about the phenomena that you are studying. Free yourself of the worry that you are behaving badly if you don't use officially certified scientific methodology.[7]

I trust no one will be misled into thinking that, by choosing qualitative measures over quantitative ones, he or she will escape or even reduce the need for rigorous scholarship. A couple of student "mathophobics" I know tried this, thinking they had found a shortcut to the Ph.D. Much to their surprise, they discovered qualitative measurement was more demanding than the statistical analyses they tried to avoid. A brief description of grounded theory as research method will serve as an example:

Most investigative approaches are designed to verify existing theory and are not concerned with the prior step of discovering what concepts and hypotheses are relevant to the investigation. Grounded theory proposes to *generate* theory from empirical data rather than simply test it. This is no easy task. Building a comprehensive theoretical base from the ground up requires logic, clarity, parsimony, and the capacity for integration.[8]

Qualitative methodologies emphasize description and discovery over hypothesis testing and replication. While I think social scientists will become less constrained by traditional methodologies in the future, it is clear that Ph.D. candidates cannot consider non-traditional methods without willing and knowledgeable thesis advisors. Since most of us were educated in traditional ways, classical modes of inquiry still predominate on most campuses, and as you know by now, universities are very conservative, slow-to-change places. Perhaps readers of this book will be part of a new cadre of researchers who, without discounting the contributions of traditional methods, will help the rest of us realize there is no single methodological road to the truth.

WORKING WITH YOUR COMMITTEE

Two students were discussing recent changes in the academic climate since the department had received accreditation by the American Psychological Association. Ray, an advanced student was advising a woman who had just passed quals.

> Just doing a high quality dissertation is not enough anymore, there is a whole parallel process which is highly political. *Everything* depends on the good will of your chair and committee, but mostly on the chair. If you've got a good one, I'd advise letting him run interference for you and by-pass your committee as much as possible. Don't show them your chapters until you have to; they will each have a different opinion and you'll be caught in the middle.

Managing feedback from a group of professors is one of the trickiest aspects of doctoral pursuit. Knowing when to take a stand and when to acquiesce calls for maturity, judgment, and "street smarts." I was interested to find substantially the same advice offered by two behavioral scientists in a book entitled *Surviving Your Dissertation,* in which they encouraged students to:

> circulate drafts of the dissertation to committee members as infrequently as possible and rely on the wisdom and support of your chairperson for major input and guidance. Whether or not this strategy seems appropriate should depend in part upon your assessment of the political climate of your department.[9]

UPDATING THE PROPOSAL

At this point you begin to reap the benefits of all the time and thought that went into the formal proposal. The first three chapters of your dissertation will be essentially the same as the proposal insofar as structure and content are concerned. Most of the modifications will hinge on the fact that the proposal was written before the investigation was conducted, while the dissertation is written afterward, a report of what you did and how you did it.

The first and most obvious change is simply an editing job, changing all tenses from future to past or present. In addition to changes in tenses for all three chapters, you will need to consider the following:

Chapter 1: Introduction

With insights gained from actually conducting the study, reexamine the theory out of which your hypotheses emerged. Can the rationale for posing research problems be more clearly stated? Are variables defined in such a way that relationships you found among them appear clear and logical? Have you introduced new terms or subsidiary questions since writing the proposal that need to be addressed now? Do the limitations you envisioned at the start need to be reconsidered in light of outcomes?

Chapter 2: Review of the Literature

Now you are sure which references pertain directly to your investigation and which are tangential. In addition, you probably have discovered new citations that shed too much light on your own problem to be ignored. Most students find some reorganization of this chapter necessary to sharpen its focus. The purpose of the chapter is to call the reader's attention to studies that have gone before and to provide a rationale for your problem and for the way you have decided to pursue it.

Chapter 3: Method

The Method chapter typically requires the most extensive revisions of all, as you move from what you planned to do to what you actually accomplished. While one hopes there are no major discrepancies between plan and implementation, it is almost certain that small adjustments had to be made to instruments, treatments, data management, statistical methods, materials, or the handling of subjects.

This is the place to describe your sample population in sufficient detail to allow readers to judge for themselves how representative it was of the population. State the number of dropouts (if any) and tell how the dropout phenomenon was treated. Did you debrief subjects who stayed in the investigation, as well as those who left? What did participants say about their experiences and what did you learn for the next project?

List in sequence the series of events that led to your findings and subsequent conclusions. Describe each event in detail: who was involved, what happened, when and where it occurred. Include the results of any pilot study. Explain and defend your research design and all statistical analyses in the light of underlying assumptions and specific objectives.

MAKING SENSE OUT OF ALL THOSE DATA

With the computer spewing out p values, t and z scores, f ratios, and multiple r's, it's easy to feel inundated with statistics. Before interpreting results, refresh your memory about the function of the statistics you used by referring to a stat text or the software package you used to conduct the analysis. I have found software packages especially helpful at this point because they tend to be very succinct.

A statistical consultant can interpret the numbers for you, but it is your job to explain what the numbers mean. Report summary findings first and do this in plain English. Instead of saying, "The main effect was significant, $F(847) = 17.29$, $p < .001$," as was the interaction, see table 9," it is far better to say, "Contrary to expectations, older counselees were more apt to report progress in dealing with phobic reactions, $F(847) = 17.29$, $p < .001$, than younger ones, as shown by the significant interaction between counseling interventions and age of counselee, $F(1,896) = 10.03$, $p < .001$." Have some consideration for your readers, by not assaulting them with too many statistics. Yes, even committee members who are used to scrutinizing numbers, can be overwhelmed. Keep graphs and figures simple and straightforward in the main text and save those tables filled with interminable numbers for the appendix. Pictorial representations of findings, although supplemental to the written word, must be self-explanatory so the reader isn't forced to refer to the text in order to understand them. In other words, tables and graphs must stand on their own.

WRITING THE CONCLUSIONS SECTION

Before writing the conclusions, go back to the introduction and review your statement of the problem. See if a slight change in wording will clarify the questions now that you have the answers. Then speak directly to the central concerns: "The primary hypothesis, 'Women suffering from Human Immunodeficiency Virus (HIV) infection are more reluctant to seek medical help than are men suffering from HIV,' was supported. The secondary hypothesis, 'Women at highest risk for HIV infection are more apt to be poor, urban and from ethnic minorities, than their male counterparts, was also supported, although age turned out to be a confounding factor." Briefly cite the evidence supporting your conclusions and describe how the variable, *age*, affected the secondary hypothesis but not the primary one. Discuss this phenomenon and offer explanations to account for it.

By this stage in your academic career, you have learned the wisdom of using what a university press director calls the "cowardly conditional," satirized in Chapter 5. Terms such as *likely, probably, apparently,* and *the evidence suggests* are defenses against aggressive dissertation committees who are quick to challenge the slightest overstatement. Although such qualifying terms can be carried to ridiculous extremes, these and other non-causal phrases are important because they describe linkages among variables while avoiding connotations of cause and effect. Such precautions are frankly self-protective, but they are also honest because the probability of rejecting or confirming a hypothesis never equals unity. Potential for error always lurks somewhere in the long journey from the inception of the idea to the testing of its merit. You will have to defend your conclusions more intensely than any other part of the investigation, so it behooves you to be careful of claims not supported by evidence, unless you clearly label them speculation.

Point out weaknesses before someone else does. Self-correction is a fundamental precept of scientific research; it is part of the ritual of doctoral pursuit and, strange as it may seem, a good way to demonstrate scholarship. Strike a balance between overemphasizing flaws in your study and sounding either apologetic or defensive. Browse through journal articles in your discipline to see how experienced researchers handle this.

The importance of the "so what?" question came up in the previous chapter on the dissertation proposal and is a logical extension of your Conclusions. You've collected and analyzed what seems like mountains of data, you've found relationships among some variables and failed to find them among others—so *what*? What do these outcomes mean for the verification of basic theory, for policy-making decisions, and for practice in your particular field of study? The livelier and more timely the issue you have tackled, the easier it is to address the "so what"? question.

Roads Not Taken: Implications for Further Research

Nearly as interesting as the answers you found are the questions you raised. In the world of research, questions are as important as answers and the complexities of human behavior are such that any single project barely taps the surface of additional possibilities. Undoubtedly, there were forks in the road where you could have taken another route. Almost certainly, there were constraints imposed on your inquiry that if removed might produce different outcomes, and you have thought of extensions of your investigation that are worth pursuing. Suggestions for further study can be very helpful to other researchers and for you later as a junior faculty member, looking for research ideas to test and publish.

THE DISSERTATION ABSTRACT

This is the time to write the dissertation abstract, even though some changes may be required as an outgrowth of the oral defense. Generally, changes at this point are minimal—modifications in wording here, redesign of a table there—nothing to refute main findings or conclusions. These few paragraphs are a culmination of years of intellectual effort that brought you to this point in your academic life. Write them thoughtfully.

The abstract, as well as bound copies of the complete dissertation, are given to all committee members in plenty of time for the final orals. If your graduate school is a member of the University Microfilms International publishing program, the rules specify that your abstract must consist of 350 words or less. It will be published in the *Dissertation Abstracts International* and indexed in the *Comprehensive Dissertation Index.*

After successful defense of your thesis, you may want to copyright your work. For a small fee, this can be done through University Microfilms International, or directly with the U.S. Copyright Office, Library of Congress, Washington, D.C., 20559. Your dissertation chair or someone in the graduate division of your university can help you decide which route is better in your case.

One challenge remains, the defense of the thesis. Not all universities require it. Some academics see it as an archaic leftover from medieval times when students did most of their work with very little faculty supervision.

So far, those who insist it is more than simply a rite of passage are persuasive. Scholars must be able to defend their intellectual positions orally if they are to survive in the "challenge and defend" climate of the modern university, they argue. Since most institutions of higher learning require you to face this final challenge, the next chapter is devoted to a discussion of ways to help you prepare for it.

SUMMARY

Careful budgeting of your time will pay off handsomely; save the most critical tasks for when you're fresh, and the routine ones for when you are less alert. Time is more important than ever before in your academic career because of the inverse relationship between the time-to-degree and the probability of finishing.

The more familiar you are with your *raw* data, the better you will be able to spot discrepancies and save yourself from backtracking to correct mistakes. Descriptive statistics give a good picture of raw data. It spotlights potential errors and gives you an overview of the shape of the data and direction your analysis is taking.

In this chapter, I discuss the pros and cons of several data-gathering techniques and suggest ways to improve response rates and to manage data efficiently. I note the obvious, that computer literacy is a modern imperative, needed to analyze quantitative data and also as a word processor. Statistical packages accomplish in seconds what used to take days or weeks to accomplish, but their efficiency may tempt you to let the program make your decisions for you, leading to less-than-optimal results. Several researcher's dilemmas (missing data, subject dropouts, unsupported hypotheses, and Type I errors) are presented along with suggestions for dealing with them.

The growing acceptability of qualitative methods offers greater flexibility in investigating human behavior, although it may be more difficult to find a willing and experienced sponsor. Be warned, however, that while qualitative methodology emphasizes description and discovery over hypothesis-testing and replication, it is equally rigorous and offers no short cuts for "mathophobics."

The Conclusions chapter will receive closer scrutiny than any other part of your dissertation. You can't measure everything, so like all research, your study will have weaknesses. Pointing out the limitations in your own work is not only good science, it is good strategy and a part of the doctoral ritual. Strive for a balance between sounding too apologetic and overly defensive.

NOTES

1. Actually, this is an old Amish saying from our familiar friend, *Anonymous.*
2. Miller, Delbert C.: *Handbook of Research Design and Social Measurement,* 5th ed. Newbury Park, Sage, 1991. This is a comprehensive collection of statistical methods, measurement instruments, and data gathering-management techniques for basic, applied and evaluation social research.
3. Kaplan, Oscar J., *The San Diego Union-Tribune,* Sunday, September 13, 1992.
4. As an advisor of students in clinical and experimental psychology, Yates presents a good case for using subject dropouts in the statistical analysis as a dependent variable because they are logically part of the experiment even if they didn't complete their participation. See Yates, Brian T.: *Doing the Dissertation: The Nuts and Bolts of Psychological Research.* Springfield, IL, Charles C Thomas, 1982, p. 141.
5. Cohen takes issue with the "Fisherian faith" that science proceeds only through inductive inference achieved chiefly by rejecting null hypotheses, usually at the p <.05 level. Yes-no decisions based upon rejecting the null are appropriate for agronomy, (Fisher's discipline) where a decision must be made to plant or not to plant, but not for the less decision-oriented development of scientific theories. See Cohen, J.: Things I have learned (so far). *American Psychologist, 45:*1304, 1990.
6. In the same article quoted above, Cohen makes a plea for more extensive use of descriptive statistics and notes that hypothesis testing has been greatly overemphasized in social science disciplines. He recommends a book by John Turkey:

Exploratory Data Analysis, Reading, Addison-Wesley, 1977, as an "inspiring account of how to affect graphic and numerical analyses of the data at hand so as to understand them."

7. Bevan also criticizes a slavish adherence to narrow, often trivial, mostly routine research projects that now dominate the landscape of research enterprises. Bevan, William: Contemporary psychology: A tour inside the onion. *American Psychologist, 46*:475, 1991.

8. Glaser, Barney G. and Strauss, Anselm L.: *The Discovery of Grounded Theory.* Chicago, Aldine, 1967, pp. 1-11. These authors argue that, while students are taught to master theories and test them in small ways, they aren't encouraged to question the theory as a whole. They claim the grounded theory research doesn't take a genius to generate and is a legitimate undertaking for students

9. Rudestam, K. E. and Newton, R. R.: *Surviving Your Dissertation: A Comprehensive Guide to Content and Process.* Newbury Park, Sage, 1992, p. 132.

Chapter 7

DEFENSE OF THE THESIS

Your dissertation is your baby, and like any parent you want to protect and nourish it. By now, however, you've discovered that your offspring also has godparents, aunts, and uncles, all of whom have something to say about its upbringing. These "relatives" are not always tactful, not always right, but they are always in charge. Until you have passed the final oral, they have a rightful claim on your infant.

Consider the case of Chuck, a candidate in business administration, the first in his family to go beyond high school, and something of a celebrity in his small southern town. Accustomed to unflagging support, he was astonished when, during his oral defense, one committee member began to attack the appropriateness of a co-variate he was using in his study of business practices.

I still don't know why Dr. G. waited until my defense to object to cultural values—he never said a word against this variable all the time I was running data. He first asked me to define *cultural values*, and then said, with much sarcasm, maybe I should try for a Ph.D. in sociology instead of business. I sat there dumbfounded, not knowing what to say!

I could tell my chair was not happy but she let me define the theoretical basis for this variable and explain why it was critical to my study. I thought I was doing pretty well when all of a sudden she interrupted me and asked me to leave the room.

Outside in the hall, my first thought was that I'd had it; they'd either fail me outright or make me start all over again. Then as my panic began to subside a little, I got mad as hell! I said to myself it was pretty late in the game for this to happen. Surely my chair wouldn't let that SOB get away with whatever it was he was trying to get away with.

134

I'd love to know what they said when I was out of the room. When they called me back in everybody acted as if nothing had happened. The next time I left the room it was only about five minutes until my chair came out with a big smile on her face, shook my hand, and called me "doctor."

What happened to Chuck was clearly an abuse of power. It didn't hurt him in the long run because his chair saw to it that he didn't suffer at the hands of an unreasonable committee member. I hasten to say this is not typical, although it happens more often than it should. Most criticisms by committee members are reasonable and can be resolved in an open discussion in front of the candidate—not behind closed doors as in Chuck's case. When there is an impasse, it is the chair's obligation to work it out.

It is extremely rare for candidates to fail final orals and it is becoming even rarer. Most committees won't let you get this far if something is seriously wrong. Those students seen as unlikely to make it are discouraged from continuing long before the final hurdle. In those few cases where failure occurs at this late date, it is almost always because the candidate has forced the issue, insisting he is ready for the defense when he is not.

Knowing that outright failure is unlikely, you still may feel awfully vulnerable, especially in settings where tradition requires putting you through a relentless, even ruthless, interrogation. If you know this ahead of time, simply accept it as part of the academic games people play and resolve not to let it throw you off balance. At the end of the exam they will all smile at you and may even take you out to lunch!

Does there have to be unanimity for the candidate to pass? The Council of Graduate Schools reports various patterns. "Almost all universities require more than a simple majority to pass the candidate. Some specify that a single negative vote fails, some that two or more negatives fail the candidate."[1]

It is highly unusual for anyone to have their dissertation accepted without any modifications at all. Editorial changes, substantive changes, and in some cases, supplementary research, are generally suggested in good faith, to improve the quality of the research.

How Dissertation Modifications are Handled

Even fairly extensive modifications are generally handled informally by having the candidate submit the revised manuscript to the person who raised the issue, and then to the chair for final approval. Some committee members are more than willing for the chair to approve all agreed-upon changes, while a few want to see for themselves that the revisions they have specified are completed to their satisfaction. In any event, be sure that your chair has the final word.

Your Right to be Included in the Negotiations

Remember, you don't have to just sit there passively, agreeing to anything and everything that is put before you; you have a right to be a participant in the negotiations. Although suggestions are nearly always intended to improve your study (not to hassle you), not all are equally deserving of implementation. I have seen students so anxious to please that they took on months of additional work which actually did little to enhance the quality of the dissertation. Chairs should protect their students from unreasonable demands, but some are timid and others tenacious when it comes to arbitrating differences. This is another instance when having a strong, respected chair, with whom you have good rapport, is an enormous advantage.

As noted at the end of the previous chapter, there are differences among institutions regarding the value of the oral defense in modern times. Some don't require it in any form, others view it more as a social formality than as an examination, while the majority maintain it plays an indispensable role in the metamorphosis of student to scholar.

Most academics who insist the final oral is an important part of process remind us that the academy has a long and honorable oral tradition which is worth preserving for its own sake. Scholarship, they claim, is more than the written word, it also entails oral expression: in the classroom, in university governance, in informal encounters with colleagues, and in the wider public forum. The better arguments are articulated, the more persuasive speakers will be. Some go so far as to speculate that those in opposition are more interested in saving faculty time than in giving doctoral candidates a valuable culminating experience.

SPANISH INQUISITION OR PIECE OF CAKE?

Long before you schedule your orals you will have determined how seriously your department takes the defense of the thesis. Unless your thesis advisor tells you it is only a formality, and even if your friends say it is a piece of cake, prepare yourself, if not for the Spanish Inquisition, at least for an intellectual debate in an adversarial atmosphere.

Worried about "overpreparation?" For years I have heard students talk about this phenomenon, but I have never seen a case where too much preparation presented any kind of problem. Perhaps these students were remembering how dysfunctional it was to cram for a midterm or a final in their undergraduate days. Cramming is a tactic used by the ill-prepared and is, in itself, anxiety-producing. It doesn't work, not because last minute studying is necessarily bad, but because it cannot make up for the failure to work consistently throughout the pertinent period.

So forget about overpreparation. You simply cannot know your own research too well, nor can you practice your presentation too often. The worst that can happen is that you could feel slightly let down after a successful defense because, compared with the time and effort invested, the final trial seemed relatively easy. Recognize the letdown for what it is and celebrate your victory.

Victory, however, is not yet at hand, so let's get back to our discussion about preparation.

The best antidote to anxiety is knowledge—knowing what to expect. Ask a friend if you can be a spectator at her orals. This will give you a glimpse of the procedures and show how she handled the questions put to her. It will also give you a sense of how rigorously the examination is conducted in your department with those particular examiners. This is not to say that all defenses are alike, of course, even with identical examiners. Much depends upon the topic, the candidate, and the vagaries of the moment. Ask if you can attend, but be sensitive to your colleague's feelings on the matter. Some people want friends there as a support group, while others consider them a distraction and potential source of embarrassment.

Arrange a Mock Defense

With the exception of a careful review of your study and its implications, there is no better way to prepare for the oral defense than to
arrange a mock exam with other doctoral students in the role of examiners. The beauty of the mock defense is that you can experiment with
different ways of responding with no penalties attached. In the safety
of your collegial group you can take back your first answer and try to
be more articulate on a second or third try. The pace of the real thing
is much faster, of course, yet even there you can slow it down occasionally by saying, "Let me rephrase my answer," or "Let's see if I can
tackle that question over again from a different angle."

Doctoral students make excellent examiners, even if they only read
the Abstract and listen to your summary. They will be just as tough on
you as the faculty, keeping you on your mental toes without the risk
that accompanies the real thing. They won't anticipate all questions,
but I think you will find them remarkably astute in analyzing major
points and ferreting out weaknesses. Best of all, they have a keen interest in your performance because of their own upcoming orals. This
"dry run" is splendid preparation for you all. It is one of those happy
occasions where everybody wins, as the following example will illustrate.

David had finished an MA in political science and was considerably
younger than the other Ph.D. students in the Political Science
Department. His politically conservative orientation in a strongly liberal department set him even further apart from the others. His proposal had been labeled "shaky," (more on ideological than substantive
grounds, in my opinion), by two influential faculty members, each of
whom refused to sponsor his dissertation.

Despite this inauspicious beginning, David eventually found a sponsor in the person of Dr. B., a senior professor with a long and distinguished career who was just stepping down from the department
chairmanship. Secure professionally, Dr. B was not worried about taking a chance with an offbeat dissertation and, in addition, he had a
good deal of empathy for David. Under his benevolent leadership,
David blossomed and was writing the final draft of his dissertation.
Then disaster struck! Driving home late one night David was involved
in a terrible automobile accident.

> I began to think I was jinxed, for sure! Even worse than the pain was
> my loss of self-confidence. Dr. B kept in touch with me in the hospital

and without his encouragement I might have given up on the dissertation. Anyway, by the time I was well enough to take my orals, about half of the students I knew had completed their research and defended. As kind as Dr. B. was, I knew he wouldn't go easy on me just because I was the original "hard-luck kid."

Actually, it was the students who helped my self-confidence the most, especially at the last. Two people I knew only slightly rounded up three people I didn't know at all and this group put me through a mock oral to end all mock orals! They asked things I would never have thought to ask myself. You've heard of the third degree, well, this was more like a seventh degree! Anyway, a week later, I passed with only minor revisions and got my Ph.D. last June.

WHO WILL BE THERE?

In addition to your committee of three or four people, there may be one or two visiting examiners from outside the department or university. The graduate division of your university may send someone, as a kind of quality control for academics! You may know all, one, or none of these visiting examiners. Some departments have a policy of "open orals" where any interested professor may attend, although it is customary to notify the committee chair ahead of time. Your chair may not inform you of expected visitors unless you ask. Don't worry about having a large audience, however, because profs who aren't required to attend have little incentive to do so unless your findings are extremely interesting or controversial.

GETTING READY

Make an appointment with the chair of your dissertation committee and ask what to expect in general, as well as any specific questions you may have in mind. Thesis advisors want their candidates not only to pass, but to do well. They are motivated both by concern for their protégés and by enlightened self interest. When you do well, it makes them look good. The more promising a student you are, the more likely your chair is to put you through your paces just to show you off to her colleagues!

Look through your notes of meetings with committee members and browse through previous dissertation drafts for comments written in the margins. These are good places to find clues about each committee member's particular concerns and interests. Also, think back on questions you heard at a friend's defense as well as those put to you at your mock defense. The specifics will vary with the focus of the study, but there are archetypical questions that are asked of nearly every candidate; we will get to those shortly.

The Setting

Exams are usually held in a seminar room on campus. Locate this room ahead of time, find a time when it is empty and familiarize yourself with the ambience. Select a spot where you'd prefer to sit, probably with your back to the windows and with the light on the faces of your questioners. (If you are the first to arrive on the day of the exam, you are likely to be able to sit wherever you choose). As soon as the date of your defense is scheduled, arrange for any equipment you might need such as a chalkboard, easel, or overhead projector. If you can have equipment delivered the day before, you'll have a chance to see that everything is in working order.

Plan to dress comfortably, but appropriately, and bring a bottle of water, coffee, or soft drink to moisten a dry throat and give you reason to pause to consider your responses. Bring an extra copy or two of your last rewrite for examiners who might have forgotten them and have enough copies of the Abstract for everybody.

That Very Important Summary

Practice delivering a brief (15 to 20 minutes) summary in this room, if possible. It is helpful to have an audience, but if you can't rope anyone into service, practice in front of the mirror at home. Do this enough times to be nearly letter perfect in your first brief overview, but don't try to memorize beyond those introductory words. Memorization will only focus your attention on the presentation instead of upon the research, and spontaneity will surely suffer. Important segments of your report will come to mind almost verbatim anyway, simply by virtue of the fact that you have written and rewritten them so many times. Plan to include in your summary the research problems and hypotheses, an explanation of how you addressed them, and what you found. Mention important limitations or qualifications of your findings without going into detail at this point. Very briefly discuss implications of your study for theory, policy, and practice.

Since your research was conducted in pieces, the summary is a way for you (and others) to view it as a whole. The summary is longer and more detailed than the Abstract, yet serves a similar purpose in that it extracts from the dissertation its most essential elements. It also has an important psychological function . . . it eases you into the discussion and helps you over your initial nervousness.

A Little Nervousness is Acceptable

While on the subject of nervousness, remember Tom whose story I related in Chapter 1? The outcome of his proposal hearing was nega-

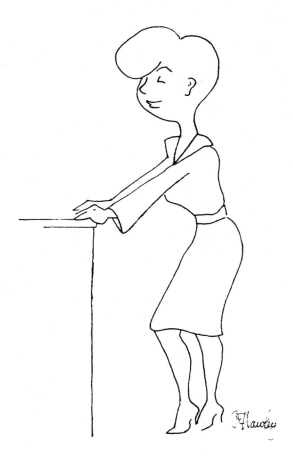

tive, primarily because he had made last minute changes, but in part because he was much too *cocky*. It doesn't hurt to reveal a little nervousness around the edges of your basic self-confidence! As devious as this may sound, it shows that you regard this occasion with the respect it deserves. Faculty are accustomed to nervousness (and wonder about its absence), but perceived *arrogance* on your part is likely to elicit challenges, if only to show you that you don't know everything yet!

Your attitude should be one of cautious confidence, non-defensiveness, and enthusiasm for your subject. Such self-assurance is appropriate, because you realize that you know more about this particular project than anyone else in the room.

QUESTIONS, QUESTIONS, AND MORE QUESTIONS!

Traditionally, candidates are encouraged to go through a summary of the dissertation without interruption before the questioning begins. When your summary is finished your chair may ask the first question, defer to a senior faculty member, or simply turn to the person next to him and ask him to start the questioning which will then proceed around the table.

There will be substantive questions and procedural questions: "What did you find and how did you go about finding it?" There will be questions on theory, philosophy, and application: "Why did you choose that particular problem and what do your findings indicate for theory and practice?" Then there is that old standby, "Of course you are familiar with Dr. Jones' (or Smith's or Roger's) work. How do you explain the fact that his findings differ so radically from yours?"

Since outcomes can be no better than the methods used to obtain them, someone is sure to ask why you used the methods you did instead of certain alternatives. Try not to get bogged down with too much mathematical or statistical detail in your answer. Simply explain *conceptually* the advantages of the analyses you used in contrast to those you might have used. Even when analyses are the obvious choices, examiners want to be sure that you understand their rationale and limitations. Self-designed measures are especially subject to scrutiny, and if you will forgive another repetition of my familiar refrain, they can best be defended with results of a pilot test.

Typically, examiners question you on passages that lack clarity. Sometimes a little "word-smithing" will clear up the difficulty, because the problem lies in your wording, not in your intellectual grasp of the problem, analysis, or results. Should your wording be due to *fuzzy thinking* it will be necessary to make more substantive changes based upon a better understanding of the matter in question.

Even when it is apparent that you haven't acquired total mastery of the subject, however, it doesn't spell disaster. As an apprentice scholar engaged in your first major project, you are given some margin for error, although this is seldom mentioned because no one wants to offer you excuses for doing less than your best. My experience with students is that they're not looking for excuses, so I remind them that no researcher, however renowned or experienced, has the final answer to any question. Even the most casual observer knows that the experts disagree.

Dealing with Weaknesses in Your Study

As you are questioned about weaknesses in your study, expect some variation of another often-asked query: "With knowledge gained from hindsight, what would you do differently if you were starting again?" and its companion, "If you had abundant resources and unlimited time, how would you redesign your study?" Perhaps you wanted to gather additional data but were hampered by insufficient funds, or maybe you realized too late that a different co-variate would have shed light on a perplexing finding. This is an opportunity for you to talk about "roads not taken" and recommend follow-up projects growing out of leads you didn't have or couldn't pursue at the time.

Two classes of questions were considered most difficult by the doctoral students I interviewed: *related research* and *statistical inference*.

Related Research. Let's assume you are asked to compare your findings to a study you have never heard of. After truthfully answering that you're not familiar with that particular research, you can regain the initiative by citing another investigation which substantiates your findings, or perhaps one in which findings differ leading to a discussion of probable reasons for these differences. The trick is to take the initiative and change the direction of the discussion to areas where you are on familiar ground, yet without appearing flustered or defensive.

If you really want to impress the committee, cite some research published after your dissertation was finished. It is worth a last-minute computer search to locate a publication hot off the press. Having current information like this at your fingertips is prima facie evidence of your commitment to the field and shows you are making the transition from student to scholar.

The oral defense is the best place in the world to be a "name dropper." Not only is it accepted, it is *required*, yet most students are content with citations from published accounts of past research. To invigorate your dissertation and stimulate your enthusiasm, try to make personal contact with an established researcher *currently* conducting an investigation in your field of inquiry. Quoting part of a phone call or letter from Dr. Distinguished Scholar at your defense enlivens the discourse considerably. While it isn't realistic to expect more than a helpful comment or reference from this person, occasionally you may be pleasantly surprised. My committee was visibly impressed with the help I had received from Dr. Fred N. Kerlinger, widely acclaimed for his groundbreaking work on measurements and statistics.[2] Not every distinguished scholar takes the time to respond as fully as he did, yet any morsel of information will enhance your study. Make the approach "cold turkey," or ask a faculty member to intercede for you. Street smart people are set apart from their fellows by their willingness to go beyond what is expected of them.

Statistical Inference. Unless your field is math, science, or statistics, you aren't expected to trace the derivation of formulas in the software that tests your hypotheses. You are expected to understand how your data were analyzed, what limits and conditions apply, and what the various statistical treatments you employed revealed about your problem. Be prepared to explain what happened to your variables during statistical analysis, how they are related to each other, and what this all means in terms of real people and events. Having a statistician on your committee is a great advantage for several reasons: she has a stake in seeing to it that your methodology is appropriate and interpretations logical, she is knowledgeable enough to query you only on matters you can reasonably be expected to know, and her very presence will inhibit less statistically sophisticated committee members and visiting profs from asking unwarranted and overly esoteric questions.

PSYCHOLOGICAL PREPARATION

Walking into the examination room you may feel quite alone and very vulnerable, but two thoughts should sustain you. First, you know more about this particular study than anyone else in the room and, second, everyone wants you to succeed. The fact that this has been standard advice to doc students for generations doesn't make it any less true. You are ready for this or your chair would not have told you to schedule it, and it is safe to say that no one will be out there gunning for you. Faculty have better things to do and besides, they save their big guns for each other!

Address all questions in the spirit in which they are asked, which isn't because the asker has grave doubts about the logic of your findings or procedures, but to determine how well you understand your own study. Comforted by the knowledge that failure at this juncture is very, very rare, resolve to take as objective a view of your ideas as possible. Achieving a psychological distance from your work at this point is not only "scientific and scholarly," it is pragmatic. Pretend, to the extent you can, that you are all colleagues sitting there conducting a critique of someone else's research.

Decide ahead of time what to do if your mind goes blank or if you sense your answer was unsatisfactory. Instead of sitting in uncomfortable silence when an answer eludes you, begin to think out loud and reason your way through the problem to a solution. This technique gets your mind "in gear" and saves you from the agony that a lengthening silence brings. This only works, of course, if the answer is hovering somewhere in the back of your mind and you are struggling with recall problems. If you really don't know, simply admit it without embarrassment or apology. It is no sin to say "I don't know," and far better to do so than to try to bluff your way through when you haven't the faintest idea what the facts are.

Another technique to get your mind out of neutral is to ask if you may return to the question after discussing the next point . . . then be sure to come back to it. If you sense your questioner is less than satisfied with your answer, simply ask straightforwardly if you adequately answered his question. If not, try again.

In the stress of the moment, it is easy to misunderstand a question or to miss completely some aspect of it. Rephrase vague or ambiguous questions so they make sense to you. In fact, I tell students to rephrase *all* questions because there is something about putting them in your own words that helps both your memory and your ability to reason. It also gives you a little extra time to formulate your answer. Then if your rewording doesn't suit the questioner, at least it will force him to rephrase his point and present it more clearly.

Finally, I will pass along the same advice given to people facing an audit by the IRS. Don't elaborate. Answer the question and then stop without speculating further. Speculation is legitimate when so labeled, but can easily be overdone in a setting like this. I agree with Ogden who notes that doctoral students tend to get carried away at their orals and give too many details that are difficult to support empirically. She also reminds readers where the real power is and advises against getting into win-lose contests. Always be courteous no matter how demeaning the questions. Even if you are tempted to say, "If you had read my dissertation you wouldn't ask a dumb question like that," find a win-win response where both of you save face.[3]

Ideally, your most important ally will be your chair, and it usually turns out this way. She sets the tone of the examination and other professors take their cues from her. Good rapport between you and your sponsor is absolutely critical all the way through the process, from proposal to final orals. The defense is the ultimate test of the quality of that relationship.

Be alert to signals coming from her, but don't expect to be "rescued" should you find yourself in trouble. Even the most dedicated student advocate won't leap to your defense because that would be condescending, tantamount to admitting you cannot defend yourself. Any assistance forthcoming from that direction is likely to be quite subtle and you will need to be alert enough to pick it up. The name of the game after all is, Defense of the Thesis, and you are the star of the event.

COMING DOWN THE HOME STRETCH

The end is in sight. Maybe that is why small barriers in the form of revisions seem to take on unreal proportions at this point. It is especially difficult for those who have prepared themselves for everything up to and including a successful defense, but not beyond. The temptation to procrastinate, or worse, to *rush through the revisions*, is nearly overwhelming.

One way to handle these temptations is to make an appointment with your chair, right away, even before you leave the examination room. The obvious purpose of this meeting is to determine what modifications will be necessary and how they will be accomplished. Not every casual suggestion made at the oral need be implemented. In fact, it is in your interest to keep changes to a minimum. Those that will clearly improve your study should be implemented, but those which will make little difference should be ignored. Your chair will decide, guided by her knowledge of her colleagues, what is important and what can safely be bypassed. As with the proposal hearing, you have a right to be part of the negotiations, so don't hesitate to interject your own ideas. Influencing the outcome will probably be much easier alone with your sponsor than at the defense. On the other hand, this is no time to risk losing the war for the sake of winning a battle.

After you and your chair have decided what is to be done, be as conscientious about tying up all those loose ends as you were with the original proposal. One more final burst of energy and the degree is yours.

SUMMARY

The seriousness with which the defense of the thesis is regarded depends, to a great extent, on the particular "style" of the department. Whether it is viewed as a social rite of passage or an intense interrogation, you can be reassured by the knowledge that few people fail at this juncture, although most have revisions to make in the manuscript.

Prepare for a minor version of the Spanish Inquisition, not a piece of cake. There is no such thing as overpreparation; you cannot know your study too well. The worst that can happen is that you may feel let down because you knew so much more than they asked you.

Attend a friend's orals and arrange for a mock defense where your colleagues grill you on your project. You won't be imposing on your colleagues because they will learn as much as you do from the experience. If possible, rehearse in the room in which the oral is scheduled to be given.

Pay particular attention to the summary of your dissertation. Strive to be nearly letter perfect in your brief overview, yet cover all the main points. Don't worry about trying to conceal your nervousness. It is expected, while its opposite, arrogance, might elicit more challenges than would typically be the case.

Questions will range from philosophical to technical, from trivial to substantive. Be able to explain why you used the measures you did and the limitations that apply. You are not expected to understand the math underlying the statistical treatment of your data, but make sure you understand the relationships among variables *conceptually* and how statistical data describes real people and events.

Preparing yourself psychologically to defend your thesis is as important as preparing yourself intellectually. Be quietly confident, stay cool, and remember two time-honored truisms: no one in that room knows the details of your project as well as you do, and no one in that room wants you to fail.

Answer the question completely, but don't elaborate. Speculation should be carefully separated from empirical evidence and used sparingly. Don't expect your chair to come to your defense; after all, you are supposed to be capable of defending yourself and your own ideas.

With the end in sight, it is tempting to procrastinate, or worse yet, hurry through required changes. Negotiate revisions with your chair (it should be easier than in the presence of the committee at the orals), and attend to each one as carefully as you wrote your proposal in the first place. You are coming down the home stretch, one final burst of energy, a few hours work, and the prize is yours!

NOTES

1. Council of Graduate Schools: *Requirements for the Ph.D.* Washington, Council of Graduate Schools, 1979, p. 13.
2. I still cherish two letters from Fred Kerlinger written in answer to some methodological problems I was having. He also gave me a rare old copy of a monograph on Q Sort Methodology. Sometimes the bigger they are, the more accessible they are, especially to struggling graduate students.
3. See Ogden, Evelyn Hunt: *Completing Your Doctoral Dissertation or Master's Thesis in Two Semesters or Less.* Lancaster, Technomic, 1991, p. 129. Ogden claims you can write the proposal, collect and analyze data, and defend your thesis within a 30 day period. Writing the report, she adds, should take no more than 20 additional days. Whether or not this time-table works for you, the book contains many good ideas for "working smart, not long."

Chapter 8

SPOUSES, LOVERS, FAMILIES, AND FRIENDS

If you're smart enough to get a Ph.D., you should be smart enough not to want one! That's what my wife says and she's got a point. I know she's tired of living on only one paycheck—hers. I know she is tired of playing both mother and father to our kids. She says I've changed and, much as I hate to admit it, maybe I have. Last night my son said, "Dad, you're not any fun anymore."

The man who said this was nearing his oral defense and had been juggling family and academic responsibilities on a limited income for five years. He is not alone. Similar complaints are echoed by Ph.D. seekers who see heretofore warm relationships grow cool because of canceled dates, postponed weekends and a sense of being left out. You're the person getting the degree, but your quest affects a lot of other people, especially those close to you. Intimate relationships appear to suffer the most.

SPOUSES AND LOVERS

Even harder than struggling with limited finances, assuming new responsibilities, and sometimes playing the role of both mother and father, is the sense of being *outgrown*. Such feelings are often not articulated, and maybe not recognized by either party. Therein lies the problem. The degree-seeker can be so focused upon the tasks ahead that it is easy to miss the fact that his wife or her lover is struggling with feelings of neglect and, perhaps, inadequacy. The comment, "I'm sick of going to parties where all you do is talk shop," may actually mean,

149

"You are entering a world where I cannot follow and I'm afraid of losing you."

As is true of many interpersonal difficulties, apparently superficial complaints can mask deeper feelings of vulnerability and resentment. In short, the *stated* problem may not be the *real* problem. You need to be sensitive to the possibility that your significant other might feel left out and/or diminished by your pursuit of a degree. Nothing is quite as boring as listening to conversations to which you have nothing to contribute and where "in jokes" predominate. This is not limited to academic settings, of course, it happens anywhere one person has strong connections with a group and the other has none.

To the extent that people are comfortable in their own skins and successful in their work roles the threat is lessened. To partners working for the common good and taking a long range view of events, anything that benefits one is perceived as benefiting the other.

TO WIVES WITH DEGREE-SEEKING HUSBANDS

The "times, they are a-changin'." But even in the twenty-first century, when women seek the doctorate it puts more pressure on the marriage than when men seek the same degree. For one thing, men often feel ill-equipped or otherwise reluctant to take on domestic tasks as this quote from Bernie illustrates.

> I got sick and tired of being a house-husband. I'd have dinner ready when Lucy got home and she'd eat quickly and spend the next few hours on the phone or at the computer. She never came to bed until midnight – needless to say, our sex life went to hell. Then one day, I heard her on the phone laughing about how I'd ruined the roast. Our marriage was already in trouble and that was the last straw. Our divorce will be final in a couple of months.

Obviously, Bernie's outrage was not so much that Lucy had criticized his cooking, but that he felt generally unappreciated. Marriages can tolerate this kind of additional stress for short periods, providing that husbands who step in to fill the void feel appreciated. Husbands should not be held to Martha Stewart standards. Overdone meat, unmade beds, white socks turned pink in the wash, or whatever violations of good housekeeping principles occur should be gracefully tolerated and never mentioned. Dust off your sense of humor and keep your criticisms to yourself.

TO HUSBANDS WITH DEGREE-SEEKING WIVES

Women have been earning PHT degrees for years. *Putting Hubby Through* is not viewed as an inappropriate role for wives, but when things are reversed it can get difficult. No matter how efficient a woman may be, she cannot conduct household business as usual and pursue the doctorate at the same time. Nothing will run as smoothly as before and you may miss those little extras that made your life so comfortable Even if you can afford to have clothes sent to the laundry, can eat most dinners out and have a cleaning lady, there are things only parents can do. You may have to take your wife's place in the ride pool schedule, help kids with homework, attend parent-teacher conferences, and do bath-time duty at night.

As important as practical support is, your wife needs your emotional support even more. After having extolled the independence of women today, I would be less than candid if I didn't present her psychological needs as well. Of the hundreds of married women doc students I interviewed in universities across the nation, the large majority emphasized their need of emotional support from their husbands. I quote Dolores, a Latina in her forties, who said it for all women. "I couldn't have made it without Al's support. He seemed to know when I needed encouragement the most and he'd say things like, 'hang in there, you're almost home.'"

In contrast, not one male student mentioned wanting emotional support from his wife. Nevertheless, I think men need and value psychological support from their mates, but are just less likely to mention it. Still Art, a doc student in business management, came close. "Jane was a hell of a good sport when I was working for my doctorate." This captures the essence of the typical man's tribute to the woman who helped put him through graduate school.

CHILDREN WITH A DEGREE-SEEKING PARENT

I can't say there weren't occasional tears and tantrums, but I think we all got something out of Beth's academic venture. The kids are a lot more self-reliant than they used to be. Making their beds and lunches each morning didn't hurt them a bit, and as for me, I learned more about cooking than I wanted to know. But because I took over some of the things Beth used to do, I got closer to my kids and that was the biggest bonus of all.

Beth has just passed quals in Counseling Psychology and was part way through her dissertation. She told me that her husband, an executive in a growing software company thought he knew a lot about time and people management. She couldn't hold back a smile when she told me he'd experienced some important on-the-job training.

Their six-year-old daughter, Cathy, couldn't quite grasp the idea of her mother going to school. That was something only children did—grownups were supposed to be *teachers.* She was overheard saying to a friend, "We have to play outside today, 'cause mom has to write a paper." When the friend asked, "How come?" she said, "I don't know but it is very, very important."

I realize that not every family is comprised of the traditional mother, father and children. Single parents shoulder a double emotional and financial burden. This is difficult under any circumstances, but with the additional demands of doctoral pursuit, it calls for enormous effort and dedication. Somehow, people find a way.

FAMILY AND FRIENDS

Two of my most interesting interviews concerned a clash of cultures involving both family and friends. A young Navajo woman at a large southwestern university spoke eloquently of trying to live in two cultures at the same time, the Navajo way and the Anglo way. While her experience is unique, it is useful to recount because it dramatizes the adjustments many students make, although perhaps to a lesser extent.

Our culture is particularly sensitive to nuances—you can easily offend without meaning to. You can say something the wrong way, stare too directly or too long and offend people. As I said, we are very sensitive.

At the university I have learned to analyze, criticize, and be tough-minded. I have also had to live with the fact that everything I say or write will be analyzed and critiqued. It has become a way of life for me and affects all my interactions with others. Now I am less sensitive to criticism, but my Navajo friends tell me I have changed and I know they don't mean it as a compliment.

Even at home I live in two cultures. My seventy-year-old father lives with us and he is used to having his every need catered to. He wouldn't eat store-bought bread when mother was alive. When my uncle comes to visit I'm expected to treat him in the same tribal way. I fix their meals while my Anglo husband fixes his and mine. They think this is pretty strange and that I'm not behaving like a good Navajo woman. I realize I'm losing part of my culture and can't ever go back. In spite of the many advantages I enjoy now, it makes me a little sad.

In another university setting on the central coast of California, I heard a similarly moving story by Roberto, a bright young Hispanic who had also come a long way from his roots. He was the youngest of six children whose divorced mother kept the family together by having them pick cotton and fruit from Texas to Michigan. Two events changed his life. I will let him describe them in his own words.

I was in the 5th grade and remember a man coming to the field where we were picking cotton. Now I know it was the truant officer who demanded my mother put us in school full time. We had been missing the first and last months of school. The man had to speak through a translator and I remember my mother acting very worried the next few days.

A year or so later I was riding in a cattle truck with other pickers on our way to the field. It was about seven-thirty in the morning when we drove by my elementary school with a bunch of kids out in front. They were my friends but I don't think they saw me. Spotting the truck they began to yell in Spanish, "dirty cotton-pickers, dirty cotton-pickers." I never forgot this and when I got back to school that fall I asked my teacher, "What can I be instead of a cotton picker?" and she said, "You can go to college."

It didn't seem possible at that time, but later, in Jr. High, I talked with a Mexican American counselor who suggested the same thing and it began to simmer in the back of my mind. It still wasn't very real because at that time, my mother worked as a dance hall girl, keeping twenty-five cents for each dance. With five other kids to support she could have worked forever without earning enough to send me to college.

Well, as you can see, I'm here! It took two scholarships and a lot of hard work to do it. I knew I had five years to finish my undergrad education or run out of money so I was extremely goal-oriented, setting a schedule and sticking to it.

As you might have guessed, I am somewhat of a misfit in my family today. None of my siblings went on to college although they are all good people, proud and self-supporting.

None were as poignant as these two, yet there are echoes of these themes in other interviews with students from mainstream America. Growth means change and change affects relationships. It is just that simple. I haven't any words of wisdom to keep it from happening or even to make it easier. All I can suggest is for you to be sensitive to the impact of your doctoral pursuit on the important people in your life. Watch for small and subtle ways to include them and make them feel needed and loved.

SUMMARY

When you are involved in as intensive an activity as doctoral study, the equilibrium of the entire family can be thrown off balance, increasing the possibilities of interpersonal conflict. Spouses are especially sensitive to changes in your attitude and demeanor although they may find it hard to tell you when they feel left out of this important part of your life. Clearly, people differ in the extent to which they are able or want to be included. Some are interested in technical aspects, others in personalities, and some are content to cheer you on from the sidelines.

Even in these enlightened times, it seems harder on the marital relationship when the wife seeks the doctorate than when the husband does. For one thing, women are too inclined to criticize when husbands, in the effort to help, fall short of good housekeeping standards. Keep your values straight here. What is important is your mate's help, not the quality of his housekeeping skills. Learning to handle unfamiliar domestic chores is hard enough for the average man without coping with the house-husband label which has little prestige in our society.

Women who seek doctorates tend to be assertive, independent thinkers, yet they need their husband's encouragement and support (expressed as well as implicit) if they are to function at their best. Men may also value emotional support from their wives, yet they appear less likely to recognize it as a need. Since the *quantity* of your time together is diminished, it is important to make an effort to enhance the *quality* of your time together.

As time-consuming as families are, they provide an anchor in the "head-oriented" world of graduate study. They are your tie to reality, helping you keep a perspective when small problems threaten to swamp you. Children gain from having a mom or dad who is also a student. They learn that learning is important, that it is a lifetime process and not just for kids.

Whether your doctoral pursuit takes you a long way from your ethnic roots or follows a path trod by members of your family for generations, it forces you to change how you think and look at the world. Growth means change and change affects your relationships with other people for good or ill, depending upon how you handle it.

INDEX

A

Abstract, writing of, 130-131
ABD (*see* All But Dissertation)
Advisor (*see* Dissertation chair)
All But Dissertation (ABD), 1 (*see* Doctor of Philosophy)
Anderson, Martin, 29

B

Bevan, Williams, 125, 133
Blackwell, J. E., 79
Bowen, W. G., 20

C

Chair (*see* Dissertation chair)
Cerny, J., 20
Chwalek, A. R., 107
Cohen, J., 123, 132
Computer use, 113, 116–124
    data entry, 116–119
    missing values, 118
    prevention of problems, 118–119
    research problem example, 118
    results, table, 118
Construct validity, 96–97
Content validity, 96
Criterion–referenced validity, 96

D

Data gathering, 94
    instrumentation, 95
    reliability, 97–98
    response rate, 94, 115, 131
    validity, 94–97

variables, 94, 116
de Sola Pool, I., 107
Defense of the thesis, 131, 134–149
    dealing with weaknesses in study, 143–144
        related research, 143
        statistical inference, 144
    delivery of summary, 140
    examiners present for, 139
    failure vote, 135
    mock defense, 138
    modifications and revisions, 135–136
    negotiations, student inclusion in, 136
    nervousness, 141–142
    preparation for, 43, 105, 137–138, 140–142
    psychological preparation, 145–147
    questions from examiners, 105, 142–143
    setting for, 140
Dissertation
    abstract, 130–131
    chair (see Dissertation chair)
    choosing a topic for, 36–37 (*see* Topic selection)
    conducting the investigation, 112–116
        becoming familiar with data, 113
        personal interview, 115
        subject dropouts, 119–120, 132
        telephone interviews, 115–116
        tips to increase response rates, 114
        Type I error, 122, 132
        unsupported hypotheses, 120–122, 132
        use of dropouts as a dependent variable, 119
    copyright of, 43, 131
    defense of (*see* Defense of thesis), 134–135
    expectations of, 83–84
    interpretation of data, 128

modifications, 135
need to complete, 110
publication, 22
quantitative and qualitative methods, 123–125
rewards for supervising, 6
sequence of steps, 55
successful second attempt, 10
time and, 108 (see Time and dissertation)
topic selection (see Topic selection)
updating the proposal, 126–128
   basis of, 126
   editing, 121–122, 126–127
use of research assistant, 113–114
working with dissertation committee, 126
writing conclusions, 129–130
   implications for further research, 130
Dissertation chair, 55–68
  big names as, 59–60, 78
  desirable personal characteristics, 60–62, 78
   accessibility, 60
   knowledge of the field, 58
   organization, 61
   warmth and friendliness, 61–62
  desirable professional characteristics, 60–62, 68–69
  "divorcing the chair," 65–66, 79
  enlisting a chair, 70
  "full bull," 59
  professors to avoid, 62–64
  role at students' defense of thesis, 135–136
  selection by department, 58
  strategies for locating chair, 66–68
   asking faculty about faculty, 68
   consulting student grapevine, 67
   taking a class from professor, 66–67
  use of technical help, 71–73
   consultant, 71–72
   contracts with faculty and staff, 73–74
   internecine warfare, 73
   statistician, 71–72
   understanding stats, 72
  working with chair, 74–75
   giving time to read manuscripts, 77
   initiating contacts, 76
   working arrangements, 74–75
Disproportionate sampling, 91–92
Dissertation committee, 70, 84, 104, 126
  relationship to student, 78

selection committee members, 70–71
  consideration of an outsider, 71
  importance chair's input, 71
Dissertationspeak, definition, 103
Doctor of philosophy (Ph.D.)
  All But Dissertation, in lieu of, 4
  comparison student to entrepreneur, 17
  intellectual demands for, 15–19, 21–22
  dropout rate, 3–4, 10–11
  effect study on others (see Doctorate study effect on others)
  indifference of faculty, 23–24
  lack socialization for students, 6–7
  sequence of steps to, 55
  "street smart," 12, 17, 20
  terminal degree, 9
  test smarts and success in school, 16
  time needed to complete, 11
  wrong reasons to pursue, 37
Doctoral study, 21–30
  faculty indifference, 22–23, 25
  intellectual demands, 21–22
  degree as producer of research, 21
  dissertation to published book, 22
  publication in refereed or juried journal, 22
  laissez faire versus apprenticeship model, 23–24
  psychological demands, 24–28
   coping with double messages, 22–23, 26
   dangers of timidity and passivity, 27–28
   help of concerned mentor, 25
   research in humanities and social sciences, 23, 34
  teaching and research (see Professorate trends, 23)
  understanding own learning style, 68–69
Doctorate study effect on others,
  culture clash, 152–153
  children, 152
  family and friends, 152
  spouses, 149–153
   fear of being outgrown, 149

E

Entrepreneur
  doctoral candidate as, 18

F

Face validity, 96
Fishbein, 107
Full bull, 59
    definition, 30

G

Gender gap, 13–16
Glaser, Barney G., 133

H

Heuristic, definition, 113
Human subjects as sample, 93
    protection of, 100–102
    psychology classes, 93
    school children, 44, 94
    volunteers, 93

I

Intelligence
    emotional, 16
    multifaceted, 16–17
Instruments, for testing hypotheses, 95

J

Jensen, Arthur R., 49, 52

K

Kaplan, Oscar J., 116, 132
Kennedy, Donald, 31
Kerlinger, Fred N., 52,144, 148
Kraemer, Helen C., 107

L

Lemke, E., 107
Long, Thomas J., 107

M

Madsen, David, 83, 107
Mellon Foundation, 10
Mentors

lack concern regarding, 9
need for mentors, 5–6
influencing student attrition, 9–10
outgrowing, 57
relationship with student, 57
Milgram, S., 107
Miller, Delbert C., 132

N

Narad, M., 20
Newton, R. R., 79, 133

O

Ogden, Evelyn Hunt, 146, 149
Older students, 13–14

P

Parsons, P., 34, 103, 107
Personal interviews, 116
Professorate
    from student to scholar, 29–30
    grant–getting, 31
    teaching versus research, 31
Proposal writing, 81–84
    advantages of pilot study, 98–99
    dissertation expectations, 83–84
    elements of, 84–89
        abstract, 85
        cover page, 85
        method, 88–89
        research problem, 86–87
        review of literature, 87–88
        title, 85
    functions of, 81–83
        contract between student and faculty, 81
        first three chapters of dissertation, 83
        insurance policy, 82
        preparation for grant–writing, 82–83
        way to save time, 81
    human subjects, 93
    presentation to committee, 84
    research concepts, 89–93
    proposal hearing, 103–104
        adversarial relationship, 104–105
        preparation for, 104

trial run for defense, 104
research ethics and protection of human subjects, 100–101
writing style, 102–103

Q

Qualitative methods of research, 123–125, 132

R

Random sampling, 90–91
Reliability, 97–98
Rudestam, K. E., 79, 133
Rudenstine, N. L., 20

S

Sample, research population 90
Sampling bias, 92
Sampling error, 92
Self–management in academic life, 18–19
Sponsor (*see* Dissertation chair)
Steiner, 108
Sternberg, Robert J., 16, 19, 20
Stratified random sampling, 91
Strauss, Anselm L., 13

T

Telephone interviews
cost, 115–116
disadvantages, 115–116
response rate, 115
Thesis director (*see* Dissertation chair)
Thiemann, Sue, 107
Time and dissertation, 108–112

hours to work on, 108
changing pace, 111
following schedule, 110–111
time for reflection, 111–112
paid employment while working on, 109
Time–to–degree, probability of finishing, 110
Topic selection, 35–48
assumptions, 49–50
avoiding controversy, 48
criteria for, 45–48
problem statement, 48–49
sources for a topic, 39–43
strategies for seeking, 44–45
expedient approach, 44
procedure–first approach, 45
theory–based/problem–oriented approach, 45–46
timing of, 37–38
Trotter, R. J., 20
Turkey, John, 132

V

Validity
types of, 95–97

W

Wiersma, W., 107
Writing style, 102–103
defensive writing, 103
dissertationspeak described, 103
use of professional editor, 103

Y

Yates, Brian T., 107, 132